D1765324

The 7 Commitments of a Great Team

a leadership fable

The 7

Commitments

of a Great Team

JON GORDON

Bestselling Author of *The Energy Bus*

WILEY

Copyright © 2025 by Jon Gordon. All rights reserved.

Published by John Wiley & Sons, Inc., Hoboken, New Jersey.
Published simultaneously in Canada.

No part of this publication may be reproduced, stored in a retrieval system, or transmitted in any form or by any means, electronic, mechanical, photocopying, recording, scanning, or otherwise, except as permitted under Section 107 or 108 of the 1976 United States Copyright Act, without either the prior written permission of the Publisher, or authorization through payment of the appropriate per-copy fee to the Copyright Clearance Center, Inc., 222 Rosewood Drive, Danvers, MA 01923, (978) 750-8400, fax (978) 750-4470, or on the web at www.copyright.com. Requests to the Publisher for permission should be addressed to the Permissions Department, John Wiley & Sons, Inc., 111 River Street, Hoboken, NJ 07030, (201) 748-6011, fax (201) 748-6008, or online at http://www.wiley.com/go/permission.

The manufacturer's authorized representative according to the EU General Product Safety Regulation is Wiley-VCH GmbH, Boschstr. 12, 69469 Weinheim, Germany, e-mail: Product_Safety@wiley.com.

Trademarks: Wiley and the Wiley logo are trademarks or registered trademarks of John Wiley & Sons, Inc. and/or its affiliates in the United States and other countries and may not be used without written permission. All other trademarks are the property of their respective owners. John Wiley & Sons, Inc. is not associated with any product or vendor mentioned in this book.

Limit of Liability/Disclaimer of Warranty: While the publisher and author have used their best efforts in preparing this book, they make no representations or warranties with respect to the accuracy or completeness of the contents of this book and specifically disclaim any implied warranties of merchantability or fitness for a particular purpose. No warranty may be created or extended by sales representatives or written sales materials. The advice and strategies contained herein may not be suitable for your situation. You should consult with a professional where appropriate. Further, readers should be aware that websites listed in this work may have changed or disappeared between when this work was written and when it is read. Neither the publisher nor authors shall be liable for any loss of profit or any other commercial damages, including but not limited to special, incidental, consequential, or other damages.

For general information on our other products and services or for technical support, please contact our Customer Care Department within the United States at (800) 762-2974, outside the United States at (317) 572-3993 or fax (317) 572-4002.

Wiley also publishes its books in a variety of electronic formats. Some content that appears in print may not be available in electronic formats. For more information about Wiley products, visit our web site at www.wiley.com.

Library of Congress Cataloging-in-Publication Data is Available:

ISBN 9781119757382 (cloth)
ISBN 9781119757399 (ePub)
ISBN 9781119757405 (ePDF)

Cover Design: Paul McCarthy
Cover Image: © Getty Images/Flavio Coelho

SKY10101152_032825

I dedicate this book to my coach Richie Moran and teammates.

Contents

Introduction   *ix*

1 Teammates Are Forever   **1**

2 Disconnected, Discouraged, Disappointing Results   **5**

3 Commitments Are Greater Than Goals   **11**

4 A Visit to Vino   **19**

5 Commitment #1: Commit to the Vision and Mission of the Team   **23**

6 Attack a New Opportunity   **31**

7 Commitment #2: Commit to Staying Positive Together   **37**

8 Commitment #3: Commit to Giving Your Best   **47**

9 The Roller Coaster   **55**

10 Commitment #4: Commit to Getting Better   **59**

11 Love Tough   **65**

12 Commitment #5: Commit to Connect   **71**

13 The Safe Seat   **79**

14 Team Beats Talent   **87**

15 Commitment #6: Commit to Each Other   **91**

16 LOSS   **101**

17 I Am…   **105**

18 Stronger Together   **109**

19 An Unexpected Fan   **113**

20 Forever Teammates   **119**

21 The 6 Commitments   **123**

22 Commitment Recognizes Commitment   **129**

23 The Funeral   **133**

24 The Power Inside You   **139**

25 The 7th Commitment   **145**

26 Forever Impact   **151**

Book Resources   *157*
Acknowledgments   *163*
About the Author   *165*
Other Books by Jon Gordon   *167*

Introduction

When people ask me how long it took to write this book I say "over fifty years" because I feel that I've been preparing to write it my entire life. I've been on a team since I was six years old and wore the number ½ on my football jersey. I have been on countless sports teams growing up in youth sports, in high school, and eventually in college. So many of my greatest memories are from my time being on a team. I love being part of a team, and I love helping teams become more united, positive, connected and committed. In fact, one of my greatest gifts and passions is to help leaders build stronger, more successful teams.

I know there are many talents and gifts I don't possess, but when it comes to leadership and teams I see the patterns, challenges, issues, and solutions so clearly. Like a doctor, I'm able to see the symptoms and patterns of disease and prescribe the antidote. I've helped iconic companies who were merging together to become more connected in order for the merger to be successful. I've worked with countless corporate leadership teams, educational teams, healthcare teams, and college and pro sports teams. In fact, over the last 20 years I've probably worked with more business, sports, education, and health-care teams combined than anyone on the planet.

This special book is a culmination of all the experiences, time, and insights I've gained working with teams. Much of this book was inspired by true stories, including my own. Coach Richie was inspired by my college coach, Richie Moran, who passed away a few years ago. He really did tell me, "Teammates are forever" before he passed away, and he really did change my life forever. In fact, after he told me "Teammates are forever," I couldn't get that idea out of my head and knew I would write a book about it one day.

So, while this is a fictional story, I believe it resonates deeply with readers because it is based on many actual events and stories that have inspired and touched me over the years. Like so many writers, I am inspired by the people I've met and impacted by the experiences I've had on my journey. This book is an expression of the best I've learned, experienced, taught, and felt.

I'm so thankful to all the leaders, teammates, and coaches I've had the opportunity to work with and learn from over the years. They have made my life so much more meaningful and rewarding and made this book possible. Without them there is no me, and there's no 7 Commitments of a great team. I'm forever grateful, and I hope this book impacts you and your team!

If you are impacted by this book, please email me at 7@jongordon.com and let me know.

Chapter 1

Teammates Are Forever

Tim sat beside Coach Richie's bed and held his hand. It was the same hand that he shook when he was offered a scholarship to play ball for him 30 years earlier. Coach Richie's grip was different then—strong, powerful, affirming. "Welcome to the team, kid," he said with a big smile so bright that Tim knew this was the place and the coach that felt right. Tim told his mom that he was going to turn down all the other offers from other schools. This was where he wanted to go. He wanted to play for Coach Richie. Besides marrying his wife, this was the best decision of his life.

Tim cried as his old coach fell back to sleep. His sick, frail body was failing. His weak grip let Tim know Coach Richie was losing his grip on life. Tim grabbed the moist towel in the bowl on the nightstand of Coach's bedroom and wiped his dry mouth. He scanned his thin, pale face and wondered what you say to the man who gave you so much and changed the course of your life.

Coach Richie opened his eyes and said in a hoarse voice, "Thank you, Tim. I needed that. I feel like it's two minutes left in the game and I'm in desperate need of a water break." He attempted to smile but his eyes lit up more than his mouth opened. "I'm not doing too well. I don't think I'm going to win this one," he said.

"It's okay, Coach. You're fighting and that's what matters most. You're a fighter and a winner. You've always been a winner. That's what you always told me, and I get to tell you that now. Coach, you can't lose, because you've already won," Tim told him.

Teammates Are Forever

Coach nodded as best as he could. "I'm just tired. But I'm doing my best."

"I know you are," said Tim. "You always did your best, and you taught me how to do my best. I love you, Coach. You changed my life. I want you to know that. I love you so much."

Coach Richie's eyes lit up for a moment. "Remember, kid, teammates are forever. Teammates are forever," he said before closing his eyes again.

"So are coaches who change your life," said Tim as Coach fell back to sleep.

Tim leaned forward in his chair and sat in silence with his head between his knees for a while before he got up, walked out of the bedroom to the living room, and hugged Coach's wife, Patty.

"How long does he have left?" he asked.

"A month, tops," she answered, with tears in her eyes.

"I'll keep checking on him, and on you," said Tim.

"We appreciate it," replied Patty. "He always loved you so much, and it means the world to him and to me that you came to visit."

"It's the least I could do. He changed my life, and I'm forever in his debt. Please let me know if you need anything. I'm going to miss him so much."

"I know, me too," said Patty as she walked Tim to the door and gave him another hug goodbye.

Chapter 2

Disconnected, Discouraged, Disappointing Results

As Tim drove to the airport, Coach's words "Teammates are forever" kept running through his mind. He couldn't stop thinking about them. Are teammates really forever? I mean, we're all going to die, so how can a teammate be forever? It's a nice saying, but is it true?

He thought about his college teammates and how he kept in touch with some of them. He thought about how they impacted his life. Yes, he would agree that teammates are for a lifetime, but forever is a really long time. Forever is infinite. Forever is eternity. He made a voice memo in his phone to continue to think more about this and then called his old teammate Brian H, whom everyone called H. They were freshman roommates and instant best friends for life. Tim thought about how wild it was to show up to college as strangers and the next day you're living with someone who snores and will be in your wedding.

H picked up on the first ring, and Tim brought him up to speed on Coach Richie's condition. They began sharing stories about him, as his teammates often did, and recalled their favorite one, which occurred before their five-hour drive to Philadelphia for a game. The bus was about to depart when they realized that Jack, one of their best players and a senior, was not on it. Coach had several guys call him but Jack didn't answer. After about 30 minutes of waiting, Jack finally showed up to the bus wearing his sports jacket, tie, slacks, and dress shoes, and looking disheveled like he overslept.

Coach was livid but he calmly said, "Hey, big boy, what do you think you're doing? You're not on your time

7

anymore. You are on my time," before making Jack walk off the bus and telling him to go run around the track four times before getting back on the bus. Jack asked if he should go get changed in the locker room before going to the adjacent field where the track was located. With an emphatic *no*, Coach told him to run in what he had on, including his dress shoes. Fifteen minutes later Jack returned to the bus with his shirt and pants drenched in sweat and his feet aching. Coach made him sit in his sweat for the entire bus ride, and no one was ever late again.

Perhaps it was Coach Richie's military background or his unconventional style or the fact that he was a little crazy in a good way, but he always found a way to make the team better. Tim and H recalled how he eventually got a bunch of self-centered superstars who didn't really like or know each other to become a winning team.

When they hung up, Tim couldn't help but think of his own team at work. Was he helping them get better? No, he wasn't. They were going through the motions. Disengaged. Apathetic. Complacent. They were on a team but they weren't a real team. They were disconnected, discouraged, and delivering disappointing results. A colleague suggested that he give them a copy of *The Energy Bus* but unfortunately no one read it. He was at a loss of what to do. How do you get a team that is simply going through the motions to create momentum? How do you get people who are focused on their own careers to care about other team members? How do you get people excited about coming to work and focused on winning together?

Tim shook his head. He had no idea what to do but he had to find a solution quickly. Too many people were quitting, too few people were applying for jobs, and if he didn't turn things around, the company he had built from the bottom up would fall flat and fail. His competition was getting better. His business was getting worse. He had to do something. He just wasn't sure what to do.

Disconnected, Discouraged, Disappointing Results

Chapter 3

Commitments Are Greater Than Goals

That night after arriving home from the airport, Tim sat down with his wife and two teenagers at the kitchen table and told them about Coach Richie. They had met him a bunch of times over the years and knew how special he was. Tim recalled that Coach Richie wasn't just his coach for four years in college—he was his coach for life. When he moved to the big city after college and got a bartending job, Coach showed up one night to visit him. When he opened his first restaurant, Coach Richie came to visit. He even played a practical joke on Tim and told the hostess at the front of the restaurant that he was with the FBI and needed to talk to Tim because he was in trouble. The hostess raced to get Tim and when he arrived at the hostess stand he found Coach Richie laughing hysterically. It was one of his many practical jokes over the years.

When Tim's kids were born, Coach Richie came to visit. When Tim started his new company, Coach came to see their humble beginnings. Over the years they both got busy but were able to see each other at alumni events, fundraisers, and gatherings. Coach Richie always asked how his family was doing and how his mom's health was holding up. He always took the time to ask, and he always cared. It was as if the moment Tim committed to play ball for him, Coach Richie committed to being his coach for life. He was like that for all his teammates. *Committed* was the word that Tim kept referring to as he talked about Coach Richie to his family. He was committed, and he got his team to be committed.

As Tim shared various stories, he recalled a powerful experience that had a huge impact on him and the team. It was the beginning of his sophomore season. The previous season hadn't turned out the way they had hoped. They had a losing record and were frustrated because they had so much talent. On the first day of training camp, Coach Richie stood in the meeting room in front of the team.

"I want you all to write down your goals for the season," he declared. "You got five minutes to do this."

Everyone began writing in their assigned notebooks and after five minutes Coach Richie had a few guys share their goals.

"I want to win rookie of year," said Duff, a short, stocky kid from New York who wasn't short on confidence.

"I want to win a championship!" shouted Vino.

"I just want to dominate!" yelled Rogers.

"Okay, great," said Coach Richie. "You got your goals. Now I want you to rip out the page in your notebooks and crumple up the paper and throw them in the trash can over there."

As everyone threw the paper balls in the trash can, Cons asked, "Why are we throwing out our goals, Coach? We took the time to write them down. Why are we getting rid of them?" Cons was a natural leader with more leadership ability than talent, and he commanded the attention of the team like no other.

Other teammates chimed in. "Yeah, Coach, we like our goals."

"Alright, alright, just take a moment and breathe," he said, calming the guys down. "I have a good reason and if you give me a minute I'll explain. You see, every one of you has goals, and I bet they include staying healthy and having so many goals or assists, achieving certain awards, and winning a championship. And I bet if you visited every team meeting room in the country, all the other players would have the same goals. So will your goals take you to where you want to go?"

Some of the guys said yes; others shrugged, unsure of the answer and wondering where Coach Richie was going with this. "No," responded Coach Richie. "Your goals will not take you to where you want to go but your commitments will. Your commitments are greater than your goals. Goals are important, and I'm going to have you write them down in your notebook again. But then you are also going to write down three commitments that will lead you to your goals. I want to know this: What are you willing to commit to in order to achieve your goals? Now I want you to write these down in your notebook."

The energy in the room changed dramatically. A serious tension emerged, in a good way. The guys took the time to write down their goals once again and then wrote down their three commitments. When they were done, Coach asked a few guys to share one of their commitments.

"I'm going to commit to extra skills work after practice instead of going to play pool and video games," Teddy said.

"I second that," said Bussman. "Hammer says that distractions are the enemy of greatness, so I'm going to do the same."

15

Commitments Are Greater Than Goals

Everyone looked at Hammer, who smiled and shrugged. He thought he was a leader but in many ways he pushed and prodded more than he led. He seemed more focused on doing the right things all the time instead of being the right kind of teammate. "I'm going to commit to more recovery time after practice," said Hammer. "I often get injured during the season because my body breaks down. If I commit to recovery, I'll hopefully stay healthy and play for the entire season."

"I'm going to make more time to study film," said Tills. "It will help me play better and also help me be a better coach in the future because I know that's what I want to do."

After a bunch of the other guys shared their commitments, Coach Richie said, "So now you see why I had you guys do this exercise. You were excited when you shared your goals but that excitement easily wears off when you are confronted with adversity, inconveniences, and distractions. When you shared your commitments, you were more intentional, serious, and focused. Writing down your goals gives you hope, but hope doesn't wake you up at 6 a.m. for an early morning practice when you want to sleep in. Hope doesn't give you discipline. Hope doesn't pay the bills when work is required. But your commitments create a standard and if you keep your commitments and live up to the standard, you will much more likely achieve your goals. So who's ready to commit to your commitments this year!?" Coach shouted. "Who's tired of unfinished goals and losing seasons? Who's ready to commit to making this the best season possible?"

The entire team yelled back, "We are!"

"Oh, baby, that's great!" Coach roared. "You each wrote down your individual commitments, and this season I'm also going to share with you our 6 Commitments as a team and program. I've done a lot of reflecting and thinking about this. I've visited my friends and colleagues in other programs. I've talked to my former players who have built wildly successful companies thinking of every possible way to turn this program around and help you all be your best. And I've brought in Coach Amy, who is going to help you apply these 6 Commitments over the season. She's worked with some of the best teams and programs on the planet, and with her help we can go to the next level. I believe these 6 Commitments are the answer. If you stick to your individual commitments and we all decide to live the 6 Commitments, together we will become unstoppable."

Chapter 4

A Visit to Vino

Tim woke up the next morning thinking about his old teammate Vino. They hadn't seen each other in years but they shared the bond of a powerful moment as teammates their senior year. Coach Richie called them both into his office and let them know they weren't chosen as captains by the team because they weren't as popular as the other guys. But he saw them as leaders and wanted them to help lead the team, even though they didn't have a title.

It was a defining moment in their lives, and Vino would go on to lead one of the top sports marketing agencies in the world. Tim thought about how Vino was thriving, while he himself was currently struggling. He figured Vino would have some great ideas on how he could turn around his team and company. He also wondered if Vino remembered all the 6 Commitments of a team, because he could only remember a few of them and had a strong feeling they would help him turn around his company. He texted Vino and asked if he could come see him.

Vino replied immediately. "Yes. Come see me. Come to my office in the city. Just let me know what time. I've missed you, my brother." Tim felt a sense of hope. It was time to go visit Vino!

A few hours later, Tim walked into Vino's office and saw all the signed sports memorabilia and pictures of famous athletes on the walls. They hugged before doing their old teammate handshake.

"Do you remember our sophomore season?" asked Tim.

"Remember it? I live by it!" exclaimed Vino. "That was the year that changed everything for me, our team, and my future."

"Do you remember the 6 Commitments Coach taught us?"

Vino laughed. "Remember them? They've been a huge key to my success. People always talk about my culture and the reason for our success, but I tell them it's your commitments that create culture and that's why we've excelled. Sports and business—the same principles apply. The fact that my company is in the business of sports just reinforces it all and demonstrates the power of these commitments."

"I love hearing this," said Tim. "It couldn't have come at a better time. I've been coasting lately as a leader and my team and company are not doing well. I need to get us back on track. I need a refresher of the 6 Commitments. I can't remember them all. Some moments are so clear, while others are a blur. I told my family about the time when Coach had us rip up our goals and focus on our commitments. For some reason I can't remember what happened after that. My memory is foggy. Hopefully you can jumpstart my memory."

"Happy to do so," said Vino as he walked over to his desk and pulled out a notebook with "6 Commitments" written on the cover. "There's nothing I enjoy more than helping my friends and talking about commitments that last," he said as he raised the notebook to show Tim. "I'll start with what happened after Coach taught us that commitments are greater than goals."

Vino motioned for Tim to join him on the balcony overlooking the park, where they sat for hours and reminisced about the past, Coach Richie and his commitments, and the unique ideas and practices that turned wannabes into winners.

Chapter 5

Commitment #1: Commit to the Vision and Mission of the Team

After Coach Richie had each teammate share their commitments, he said it was time for practice, and they ran out of the team meeting room and onto the practice field. Coach whistled like always and shouted his favorite sayings. "It's great to be here! Oh, baby, it's a beautiful day." Then he whistled some more and motioned for the team to join him at the center of the field, where a big rope lay on the ground. He instructed half the team to get on one side and the other half to get on the other side. "Now pick up the rope," he ordered.

"Are we doing tug-of-war?" asked Antonio.

"Of course we are. What else would we be doing with this rope?" Joey replied sarcastically as everyone laughed.

"On the count of three I want you to pull as hard as you can. The losing team runs a lap around the field!" shouted Coach. He loved competition and always got the guys to compete for everything. He believed that if you loved competing, you would experience more winning.

"One, two, three, go!"

The guys pulled and strained with everything they had. It was more than running laps that was at stake. It was pride, a desire to win, and bragging rights at dinner that pushed them. After a few minutes and no clear winner in sight, Coach yelled, "Stop!" All the guys let go of the rope and dropped to the ground. They were exhausted, and their arms and legs were spent. Coach paced back and forth for a few minutes as the guys recovered.

Commitment #1: Commit to the Vision and Mission of the Team

"Now I want you to get up and all go to one side of the rope. I want you all to face the same direction and pick up the rope. Let's go!" he shouted before whistling. This wasn't his "It's great to be here" whistle, but his "Get moving" whistle. As the freshmen would learn, Coach Richie had a whistle for everything. Coach then instructed the training staff and the strength and performance coaches to go to the other, short side of the rope, face the team, and pick up the rope.

"One, two, three, pull!" he shouted, and the competition ended very quickly.

"That was too easy," said Duff.

"That's the point," Coach explained. "When you're all facing the same direction with a common mission, you're much stronger together than working and fighting and pulling in different directions. It's easier when you pull together. It's draining and exhausting when you don't. This year we all need to pull together."

Coach whistled again and told the team to huddle up in a circle around him.

"Last year we allowed too many things to divide us. Last year we weren't *one team*. This year we are going to become *one united team*. This year my job and all of our jobs is to create a team with oneness in mission and vision. A team that is divided is weak. A team that becomes one is powerful and strong. We are all going to become *one team*, face the same direction, and commit to a shared vision and mission."

Coach Amy entered the circle and said, "That's the first commitment we must make this year. What is the vision and mission you want to commit to as a team? Coach and I can tell you what that commitment should be, but it's more powerful when you all decide it as a team. We don't expect you to know what that is right now, so what we are going to do is practice. Then after practice we'll gather in the team meeting room and see if we can figure this out."

Coach Amy was a former Division 1 athlete who was a part of too many losing teams that shouldn't have lost. When she graduated and went into coaching, she made it her personal and professional quest to find out what prevented teams from being their best and what propelled them to greatness. After a short successful career as a coach, she began consulting with various coaches and teams who sought her knowledge, wisdom, and practical advice. She had a unique blend of understanding culture, leadership, teamwork, mindset, and what made players tick. She knew, however, that it wasn't how much she knew that mattered most. It was what the team was willing to do that determined their ultimate success. She was excited about the possibilities with this team but just hoped they would be willing to do the work, because Coach Richie had told her that last year was a disaster.

After practice the team and staff gathered in the team meeting room and began discussing possible visions and missions. After many disagreements among Rogers, Hammer, Duff, and H, Tills spoke up. "I think we have the answers right in front of us." He pointed to the board. "Our vision is what we want to create, and on the board I see 'one' and 'gritty' and 'competes' and 'champions.' So let's make it our vision to become One Gritty Team that Competes like Champions." All the guys nodded in unison.

"Do we all like that?" asked Coach Amy.

"Yes," they all replied, feeling good that they were making progress.

"It's a great vision," she said. "So often teams will say they want to win championships, but I think it's more important to compete like a champion, because when you compete like a champion and play like a champion and commit like a champion, you win championships more often. Teams often focus on championships but they don't engage in the process of what it takes to be champions."

"I love that," said Tim. "That's what hurt us last year. We were so focused on winning a championship we fell apart when it mattered most."

"We'll be talking more about that over the next few weeks," explained Coach Amy. Then she walked to the board and wrote "Mission" on it. "And what about mission?" she asked.

Cons stood up. "I don't know about you all, but last year was painful. I never want to go through that again. But I also know that it's not just about us. It's about every team that comes after us. So I feel like our mission should be to define this program. It should be to leave a legacy. We should be the team that changes everything, so that every team that comes after us will say *that's* the team that elevated this program. That's the team that showed what winners do and how to do it. That's the team that set the bar and inspired every team after them to raise it and go to an even higher level."

"I like it," said Coach Amy. "But that puts a lot of pressure on you all. Do you all want that kind of pressure? Do you want that expectation?"

"Yes," they all said in unison. Cons's words and mission resonated with them. Deep down it felt good to commit to something greater. They knew they could be more and achieve more than they were.

"Well, that's wonderful," Coach Amy declared. "I'm proud of you all. It's much easier to think of your own personal commitments, goals, and vision than it is to come up with a shared vision and mission as a team. With that said, I want to reiterate that it's important for you all to maintain your own personal vision, commitments, and goals. Those are essential to your success. I know you want to be great and that's a great thing. But I also know that when you focus on becoming a great team in addition to your own individual greatness, that's when you become truly great. So are you ready to commit to the shared vision and mission of the team?" she asked as she wrote them on the board:

Vision: Become One Gritty Team That Competes Like Champions.

Mission: Define and elevate this program. Set the standard and inspire teams after us to reach an even higher level.

Everyone said yes. They were fired up and committed to the vision and the mission.

Chapter 6

Attack a New Opportunity

Aweek later the team had their first scrimmage of the preseason, and it didn't go well. Duff made too many rookie mistakes. Cons led well but didn't play well. Teddy was a bright spot and played the best he'd ever played. But the rest of the team either pressed too much or were too hesitant. Hammer kept telling guys what to do, and Vino was frustrated that the team wasn't doing it. He knew they had so much more potential than this. They played with little confidence and chemistry and looked even worse than last year. Coach Richie knew it was going to be a long season if they didn't get it together.

The next morning before practice, they met in the team meeting room. Coach Amy asked, "So what went well yesterday?" Everyone pointed to Teddy.

"And what didn't go well?" she asked.

"We didn't play together as team," said Tim. "It was a lot like last year."

"We pressed too much," said Rock, who was an all-American goalie. "I think our vision and mission made us feel like we had to be the team we want to be right now. We don't want to lose like we did last year, and I think too many of us are still thinking about last year."

"That's a great point," observed Coach Amy. "You guys have to realize that change doesn't happen overnight. Don't let perfection get in the way of progress. Just because you have a big vision and mission doesn't mean you have to do more than you're capable of doing. And it doesn't mean that you play timid and afraid, either. Mistakes are going to be part of our growth as a team. Don't be afraid to make them."

Attack a New Opportunity

Coach Richie walked to front of the room, paused for a moment, took a deep breath, and stated, "I know what we have to do. We have to let go of last year and stop thinking about it. You don't create today by focusing on last year. Last year was last year. This is this year. We can't look backwards. We have to look forward."

He walked to the whiteboard and wrote "Defend" and "Attack" on it. "I found some research saying that teams that feel like they're defending something don't perform well. But teams that attack a new opportunity do great. I feel like we're a program that is always defending something. We have a lot of talent and potential so everyone expects us to win, and we have to defend our status and reputation and live up to the media hype and what people think. That leads to unnecessary pressure and poor performance. From this moment on, we are not defending anything but our goal. We're going to attack a new opportunity every moment, every game. We will not focus on the expectations others have for us. We will focus on our commitments and let those commitments drive our results. Do you hear what I'm saying?" he hollered to the team.

"Loud and clear!" shouted Vino.

"We get it, Coach, and we got you. Right, guys?" shouted Cons, imploring them to respond.

"We got you, Coach," they all chimed in.

"Great," said Coach, "because we have our first game of the season in two weeks and I want us to attack a new opportunity every day until then." Coach could feel the burden of their expectations being lifted. He knew they cared but didn't want them to carry the pressure they had been carrying. *Care but don't carry* was something he promised himself he would do as well. He felt a change in the energy of the room and knew that attacking, not defending, was going to be a key mindset shift that would make a huge difference. He would just need to remind them of this constantly throughout the season. Teaching these principles to your team is important. Reinforcing them constantly is everything!

Chapter 7

Commitment #2: Commit to Staying Positive Together

Coach Richie could feel the tension rising. Training camp was taking its toll. The guys' bodies were tired and sore. Their minds were reeling. Some were asking themselves if they were good enough to make the team. Others were worried about playing or riding the bench. Several were worried about losing their starting position. As their bodies broke down and the questions in their head got louder, they became more frustrated, irritable, and moody. Coach knew they were almost at the brink and decided today was the day to push them toward it. It would be a great opportunity to teach them a lesson that would define their season and their life. With a week left until their first game, he decided to make today the most difficult and grueling practice of training camp and then afterwards he would get them ready with proper rest for their first game of the season.

Practice began surprisingly strong. Coach cheered at the beginning of practice like usual. "Oh, baby, it's great to be here!" The guys were energized and fierce. But the more they ran and trained and did drills and scrimmaged, the more frustrated they got. As the mistakes mounted and the competition heated up, things got chippy. And then it happened. Rogers and Hammer got into a scuffle and a fight broke out with some pushing and shoving, others wrestling, and some even throwing a few punches. The coaches and support staff broke up the fight and thankfully no one was injured.

After everyone calmed down, Coach whistled, letting everyone know it was time to circle up. "Listen, men. I'm

Commitment #2: Commit to Staying Positive Together

not happy this happened. But in a way I'm glad it did. It's a great lesson for us. I know training camp has been tough. We've asked a lot of you. We've pushed you. We've challenged you. I know your bodies are tired and sore. You can't control those things. But you can control how you respond to your situation and that determines the outcome. And let me tell you, you can always respond in a positive way. You always have a choice between negative and positive. You must choose the positive. If we are going to have a great year, we must commit to staying positive together. Are you with me?" he asked, as his eyes darted left to right and he scanned his team's faces.

"Yes!" they all shouted as Duff, H, Teddy, and Bussman wiped the dirt off their jerseys and Rogers and Hammer stared at each other.

"We have to stay positive *together*," Coach yelled, emphasizing the final word. "That goes for you two, Rogers and Hammer. Together is the key. The collective positivity and belief of our team is the result of each one of you choosing to stay positive and believe in our vision, our mission, our ability to win, and each other. Your positivity, optimism, and belief matters and every day you must feed yourself in order to feed your teammates. If you don't have it, you can't share it. And since each one of you is contagious with your energy, you can affect your team with positivity or infect each other with negativity. I've seen too many teams lose their way and their seasons because of negativity. Too many allow fear, frustration, adversity, complaining, and energy vampires to sabotage their team.

There's no way I'm going to allow that to happen this year, and there's no way you are going to allow it, either. Are you with me?"

"Yes, Coach!" they responded,

"Good, because there are times we will get frustrated. We will face adversity. Negative thoughts, fears, and doubts will pop into our head. It's a daily battle, and to win the battle we must commit to staying positive together. There will be times when Duff won't be positive and he will need you, Antonio, to encourage him. And when Tim is struggling, he will need Joey to lift him up. It's a long season that's like a roller coaster. There will be ups and downs. But here's the key. Stay on the roller coaster together. Don't jump off. Don't escape. Just stay on it and keep working and stay positive together and you will ride the roller coaster to a higher level and greater success. Tell them about the NBA team, Coach Amy."

Coach Amy made her way to the middle of the circle, "Several years ago I was working with an NBA team, and they started the season 11–30. They were the laughing-stock of the league, and all the pundits and broadcasters ridiculed them. But they didn't listen to what everyone else said. They didn't focus on their circumstances. They focused on staying positive and getting better, and as a result they finished 30–11 and almost made the playoffs. I learned that a team that stays positive together ultimately has a much better chance of succeeding together."

"And tell them about that Major League Baseball team you worked with," Coach Richie said.

"Well, it was spring training, and they were tired and frustrated like you all are right now. And the guys were being really moody. So when it was my time to speak to them, I told them straight up that it's not okay to be moody. If you're moody, you can't be your best. If you're moody, your team doesn't know what to expect from you, and if they don't know what to expect from you, then they can't trust you. To be your best you must be consistently positive. I thought they were going to run me out of the locker room after challenging them, but so many of the guys came up to me and said they needed to hear that. After that moment guys weren't moody; they stayed positive and went to the World Series."

"And tell them one more, about that college football program," Coach Richie said.

"I love this story," Coach Amy exclaimed. "The coach wanted to eliminate the energy vampires so he put a picture of an energy vampire on the wall of the team meeting room. Anytime one of the players was being an energy vampire, they put that player's picture on top of the energy vampire picture. No one wanted to be on the wall. They discussed the importance of staying positive together and not allowing negativity to sabotage their team. In many ways the most important decision a team can make is to decide they will not allow negativity to keep them from achieving their vision and mission. Guys who normally became negative chose to stay positive even when they lost the first two games of the season. The media and fans were loud and angry but this team stayed positive and won the next 10 games in a row, making it to their conference championship. Once again, we see that a team that stays positive together succeeds together."

"So how do we stay positive together?" Coach Richie asked.

"That's a great question and a great point," Coach Amy responded. "It's easy to say we must stay positive, but how do we do it? It's easy to stay positive when things are going great. But the real test is whether we can stay positive when things aren't going our way. How do we stay positive through the roller coaster of a long and challenging season? Well, that's why I have a copy of *The Power of a Positive Team* for each of you to read during the season. You can pick it up before you leave today. I also made a cheat sheet for you of "5 Ways to Stay Positive" this year to give you some practical tools and mindsets to help you keep this commitment. But before Coach ends practice, I want to share with you one strategy that all of you can implement right now, throughout the season and for the rest of your life. It's appreciation, and it's the antidote to entitlement, frustration, and stress. I want you all to simply appreciate where you are, what you have, and what you get to do. Appreciate this moment. Appreciate this team. Appreciate that you get to do this. Do you know how many young athletes dream of this opportunity that you all have right here, right now? So I want you to appreciate what you have instead of worrying about what you don't. When you appreciate, you elevate your mood, your performance, and the people around you."

Coach Richie ended practice after their speech to the team and encouraged them to enjoy the day off tomorrow and then get ready to recharge and prepare for game week and their first game of the season. As they walked off the field, Rogers and Hammer shook hands and Teddy and Bussman gave each other bro hugs. Tills ran around patting everyone on the back, while H and Duff laughed about throwing and missing their punches. They knew the moment had gotten the best of them and brought out the worst in them. This lesson couldn't have come at a better time. Before leaving the facility, they picked up their books and the one-pager with "5 Ways to Stay Positive," which looked like this:

---

5 Ways to Stay Positive
Live LIGHT

1. **Love instead of fear:** Love casts out fear and it's the most powerful way to stay positive. Too often we let fear rule our mind. We fear making a mistake. We fear what people will think. We fear failure. We fear not living up to our expectations or the expectations of others. These fears often weaken us, limit us, and paralyze us. The answer is to choose love instead of fear. The minute you focus on love, fear dissipates. Instead of fearing the outcome, love competing. Instead of fearing not playing well, love playing. Instead of fearing your opponent, love the battle. Love the moment.

Love the opportunity you have to play this game. Love elevates your state of mind and makes you feel more confident, positive, and courageous. Love is not weak. It's strong and it makes us powerful.

2. **Inside out:** Remember the truth that the power inside of you is greater than the forces outside of you. You don't create your life from the outside in. You create it from the inside out—from your spirit, soul, passion, drive, and power within. So don't look outside at the expectations and opinion of others in the media and feel pressure. Instead, look inside and know you are more powerful than all of it. You have the power to transform your environment, your circumstances, and your team.

3. **Get to:** When you find yourself complaining or being stressed instead of thinking about what you "have to" do, realize that life is a gift, not an obligation, and focus on what you "get to" do. When you focus on "get to," you feel grateful, and gratitude moves you from entitlement, frustration, and stress to appreciation and abundance. Research shows that you can't be stressed and thankful at the same time. If you are feeling grateful, you won't feel stressed.

4. **Have faith:** When facing a challenge or experiencing a difficult situation, believe that things are going

(continued)

(continued)

to improve. Have faith that somehow, some way, things are going to turn around. Expect challenges but have an even greater expectation that you will overcome them. Trust that struggle leads to strength and setbacks lead to comebacks. Always believe that the best is yet to come.

5. **Talk to yourself. Don't listen to yourself:** Instead of listening to the negative thoughts in your head, talk to yourself and be your own greatest encourager. Instead of beating yourself up, choose to lift yourself up with positive and affirming words. You are not the thoughts you think. You are the thoughts you believe. So don't believe the negative thoughts in your head. Replace them with positive thoughts and choose to believe them.

In the back of this book you will find a link to download a PDF of five ways to stay positive.

Chapter 8

Commitment #3: Commit to Giving Your Best

After their day off and a few days of practice, Coach Richie noticed that the guys were making too many mistakes. Too many were not being consistent. Too many were not giving their best effort. As a coach, he knew there were times his team needed to be pulled up and times they needed a push. With a few days left before their first game, he believed that now was a time they needed a little push. Before practice he had the team gather in the meeting room.

"How many of you believe you can work harder than you already are?" he asked.

All the guys raised their hands. He looked around and laughed. "So what's the next question?" he asked.

"Why aren't we?" responded Cons with a tone that said he was trying to figure out the answer himself.

"Great question. Why aren't we?" Coach Richie repeated, shaking his head and laughing to himself.

"Because we are beat up from training camp," said H. "I mean, my legs feel like cement these days."

"I think it's my mindset," said Tim. "I feel a little sluggish, and then my mind starts thinking about how sluggish I feel and then, I don't know, I just don't feel light. I feel heavy. Like everything is harder than it should be."

"I appreciate you guys being honest," said Coach Richie. "I think those are definitely valid reasons, but I also know there are times you feel the same way and yet you are still able to give 100 percent. There are times your body feels like a truck, not a sports car, and I see you give your all. There is a bigger reason and it's this." He

49

walked to the board and wrote, "Care more" on it. Then he walked toward his team, whistled, and said, "To work harder, you have to care more. If you care more, you will push through the soreness. If you care more, you will give your all even when you feel like you don't have your all. If you care more, you won't just go through the motions. If you care more, you will always give your best. And that's the next commitment I want you all to make this season. I want you to commit to giving your best. Not just one time, but all the time. Not just one day, but every day. So let me ask you, can you care more so you can give more?"

"Yes, Coach!" they all shouted.

"Supercalifragilisticexpialidocious," said Coach. "I love hearing that. But let me ask you, what does it mean to commit to giving your best?"

"It means effort," responded Rock.

"Yes, effort is a huge part of giving your best. We always say 100 percent effort around here. I know you might not be at 100 percent every day based on how you are feeling but you can always give 100 percent of what you have. The more you care, the more effort you will give. But giving your best is more than just effort. I wouldn't be a good coach if I didn't tell you how else to give your best beyond effort. Do you want to know what else giving your best requires?" asked Coach Richie.

"Yes, Coach!" all the guys shouted. H was louder than all of them.

"Giving your best requires consistency," Coach Richie said as he walked to the board and wrote *Consistent* on it.

"You need to be consistent with your actions, habits, rituals, and routines. You need to be consistent with a positive attitude and show up every day and do the right things over and over again. When you are consistent with your mindset, actions, and effort, you won't make so many mistakes on the field. Right now we are struggling with consistency, and it's why you are not giving your best or being your best."

"What does it mean to be consistent?" asked Tills, who always wanted to get to the heart and meaning of what Coach said and did.

"I had a feeling you were going to ask that, Tills," said Coach, giving Tills a wink. "So I looked it up and read that consistency refers to the act of repeatedly performing an action over time. In our case it means you repeatedly get enough sleep. You fuel your body with the right foods and nutrients. You repeatedly practice and work on your skills. You repeatedly make the right play and pass over and over again. You repeatedly show up on time and do the things that help you be your best and give your best."

"Interestingly, being consistent helps you give your best, and it's also a byproduct of giving your best," added Tills.

"That's true," said Coach, knowing Tills was going to make an amazing coach one day. "And this brings us to the other part of this equation to give your best, and it's discipline. While consistency is repeatedly taking action, discipline is your will to actually do it, even when you don't feel like it. Discipline is essential for you to be

51

consistent because there will be days you don't feel like giving your best. There will be days when you don't feel like going to sleep or eating right or taking an ice bath or working on your skills, but because you have discipline, you do it. You stick to your plan, tune out distractions, and honor your commitments even when it's not convenient and easy. If you want to be a great team, you have to be disciplined and consistent. When you are consistent and disciplined you trust yourself more and your teammates trust you more."

"I get it, Coach," said Tim. "But there are days and times I'm not disciplined or consistent. My will is weak and my actions suffer. You're saying we need to be more disciplined and consistent to give our best, but how do I become more disciplined and consistent?"

"I'm glad you asked that," said Coach Richie, "because this is exactly what I was going to share with you. Too many coaches like me are always telling their players to be disciplined and consistent, and yet we don't share the driving force behind the will and the action to do what must be done. And what is this driving force? It is devotion. When you are devoted to something, you will have more discipline. Trying to be disciplined without devotion is like swimming upstream against the current. It's like walking uphill. It's a grind and a chore. But when you are devoted to something, discipline is much easier. You want to practice. You want to improve. You want to work hard. You want to excel. You want to master it. You love it and want to be great at it. No one had to force the all-time greats in sports, music, art, and literature to work on their craft. They were devoted to it, and that drove their discipline. Devotion gives you power. It causes you to care more. Because you care more, you give your best effort. Devotion and caring more drives your discipline, and being disciplined each day leads to you being consistent and all of these combined lead to you giving your best."

Coach went to the board and wrote an equation for them:

$$\text{Devotion} + \text{Care More} + \text{Effort} + \text{Discipline} + \text{Consistency} = \text{Giving Your Best}$$

"Does this make sense?" asked Coach Richie.

"Yes," said Tim. It finally made sense. Finally, someone explained how to actually be disciplined instead of just yelling that you need more discipline. Finally, someone explained what drives someone to be disciplined and consistent. It wasn't just about action. It was tapping into the power of love and devotion that drove their action and commitment, and that really resonated with him and the team. Now they had to ask themselves a bigger question: *Were they truly devoted and committed to giving their best and being their best?*

Chapter 9

The Roller Coaster

Coach Richie's words and commitments must have struck a chord, because during the first game his team outworked, outhustled, and outplayed their opponent and cruised to victory for their first win of the season. After winning they celebrated and danced in the locker room and vowed to win their next game, which they did four more times for a record of 5–0. They started the season with a bang and everyone took notice, including members of the media, who wrote articles about their hot start to the season. The guys shared the articles and praise with each other and quickly began to believe the hype more than they focused on their commitments. Coach Richie had a feeling about what was going to happen next but he didn't say a word. He told his staff that sometimes the best teacher is experience, and we have to let others go through it to learn from it. And then it happened sooner than he thought. Complacency and arrogance replaced commitments, and they lost the next two games in a row.

A season is like a roller coaster, with ups and downs, and when you're up you can't get too high on yourself. And when you're going down the roller coaster and feel like you're crashing, you can't jump off and escape. You just have to stay on the roller coaster and focus on your principles and commitments. If you stay positive and stay the course, stay true to your principles and convictions, you will ride that roller coaster back up to greater heights and success once again.

Coach Richie knew exactly what his team needed to hear and what the next commitment was that he should teach them. He decided he was going to do it after practice today. Every team had issues and challenges along the way. The difference between bad teams, good teams, and great teams was that the bad teams ignored the issues, the good teams addressed the issues, and the great teams got better and stronger because of the issues. He hoped this team would do what great teams do, and he was going to do everything in his power to make that happen.

Chapter 10

Commitment #4: Commit to Getting Better

After practice the guys took their seats in the meeting room and Coach Riche held up a newspaper. "Hey, big boys! Don't believe the press clippings. They will tell you that you're better than you are and worse than you are. Today's paper wraps tomorrow's fish. It means nothing," he said as he crumpled up the paper and threw it into the garbage. "Commitments are everything! You guys have been more focused on what everyone is saying about you than on getting better. You got complacent and arrogant very quickly, and look what happened. You were 5–0. Now you're 5–2. Guess what? Excellence doesn't care what our record is. Excellence doesn't care what the score is. It only cares that you are getting better. I only care that we are getting better. From this moment on, I want us to commit to getting better every moment, every practice, every game. Can we do this?"

"Yes, Coach!" the team cheered.

"Great," said Coach as he clapped his hands together. "Complacency and arrogance are the enemies of great teams. What made you good in the past will not make you great in the future. It's not just about giving your best effort. It's about giving your best effort to continually improve and get better. The good news is that we are early in the season and still have a lot of time to turn this lesson into a great opportunity to get stronger and better. So how do we continually improve?"

"We focus our minds and efforts on continuous improvement each practice," said Tim.

Commitment #4: Commit to Getting Better

"That's a great start," answered Coach. "It all starts in the mind. So let's make sure each one of you is focused on getting better. What else?"

"We have to challenge each other," said Tills. "When one of our teammates is not giving their best or working to get better, we have to push each other."

"Great one," said Coach. "I want us to be a family who loves each other, but we must be a real team that challenges each other. I can tell that you guys don't want to confront your teammates when they're slacking. But if you don't say anything, we won't get better. From now on we're going to do a 'Tell the Truth' exercise after practices and games where we tell the truth about our effort and performance and share how we can get better. We are going to ask three questions after practices and games."

Coach walked to the whiteboard and wrote down the questions:

1. What went well?

2. What could we do better?

3. What did we learn that will make us better?

"This is going to help us hold each other accountable to our commitments and make sure each person is giving their best and working to get better. If you see it, reinforce it and recognize each other. If you don't see it, call it out and address it."

"It's called difficult conversations," said Coach Amy. "Every team has to have them if they want to be great. Too many teams don't have difficult conversations so they stay stuck in the status quo or get worse. They don't deal with the issues that are holding their team back, so they don't rise above their challenges and circumstances. If you guys can get good at having difficult conversations and holding each other accountable, your performance and teamwork will improve dramatically."

"Does this mean we can't be happy when we're winning and celebrate our wins? We love to dance," said Rogers.

"No, not at all," said Coach. "I want you guys to celebrate and dance when you win. The fun is in the winning. But we don't get caught up in the wins. We dance, we celebrate, and then we move on to the next one as we look for ways on how we can improve and get better."

"It's called positive discontent," said Coach Amy. "You feel good and positive about what you have accomplished, but you have some discontent knowing there are things you can do to improve. As John Madden said, 'Winning is a great deodorant. It covers up what stinks about your team.' So while we might have won, let's continually look for ways we can improve so we don't cover up the stink."

"Cover up the stink—that's great advice for Bussman," exclaimed Teddy as the rest of the team laughed.

"Alright, I can tell you guys are getting restless," said Coach. "The last thing I want you guys to know is that in your commitment to getting better, it's helpful to look at every challenge as a lesson that will help you get better. In the course of a year, every team will face competition, adversity, and situations that we have to deal with. I call these obstacles "partners in growth," and they are part of our curriculum in life and are designed to make us better and help us grow. If you don't face them, you don't grow. Adversity is your partner in growth. Even people who wrong you are your partners in growth. If you are never tested, you become weak. If you don't have battles to fight, you won't become strong. Every test and rival you face is meant to make you stronger, and the tests we face as a team are meant to make us better if we choose to learn from them. We just have to commit to getting better and use both the good and the bad to make us better. See you all tomorrow for our next game and another opportunity to get better."

Chapter 11

Love Tough

In the next game, the team gave every ounce of energy, effort, and determination they had. They played hard. They were relentless. They challenged and pushed each other. They outworked and outplayed their opponent for most of the game. Yet with a minute left, their opponent tied it up and won in overtime.

The next game was another physical and emotional battle as each team took the lead and lost the lead several times. It was a game of momentum and whoever seized it took the lead for that moment, only to have their opponent come back and reclaim the lead. With a few minutes left, the game was tied and Coach Richie called a time-out.

"We are not losing this!" yelled Hammer. "Let's fight to the end. Get mad. Get angry. Do whatever you have to do to get pissed off and let's win this thing."

"Just do your job!" yelled Tills. "Everyone do your job and we'll be fine."

"Just get me the ball!" bellowed Joey.

"No fear!" shouted Rogers. "Let's want it more than they do."

Coach Richie heard the words, but more importantly he sensed what they were really feeling. They were pushing and challenging and saying, "No Fear," yet deep down they were really fearful. They feared losing more than they loved battling together. That was a conversation for another time. With a frantic huddle and only a few seconds left in the time-out, he announced, "Alright, guys. I believe in you all, and you just give your best to the end. That's all I ask for. Let's go do this."

They did give their best. They stayed positive. They battled like their life depended on it because when you are playing with fear, it does. Losing feels like death and winning is how you reclaim your life, until the outcome of the next game. They took the lead with two minutes left, only to have the other team score with a minute left. Once their opponent tied it up, Coach Richie's team got tight and began pressing too much. Hammer and Rock were not on the same page. The other team capitalized on their mistake and scored with 30 seconds left and won the game.

The heartbreaking loss meant two losses in a row. The guys sat in the locker room exhausted, devastated, and defeated. They were now 5–4 and their season was on the brink. Coach Richie knew they were at a pivotal crossroad. They would either turn it around or the season would be another disaster. He knew the guys played their hearts out and after the game in the locker room he told them he was very proud of them. Their commitment to being their best and getting better was unmatched. He never had a team work so hard and give so much. But while he didn't say it in that moment, he knew the problem was that they challenged each other more than they loved each other. Every great team needs a combination of love and accountability. Tough love is essential, but love must come first. He helped this team have a lot of accountability, but they needed more love. They were being tough on each other but to be truly a powerful team they needed to love each other. They needed to love tough.

Love tough means you love each other and then earn the right to challenge each other. Because you feel the love of your teammates, you are more open to them challenging you. If you challenge your team members but they don't feel your love, it won't be received well. But when they know you love them, then when you challenge them, it is seen and felt as an act of love. Because you love your team members, you challenge them to rise up and be their best. Accountability is essential; it just needs to be wrapped in love. Coach Richie decided that instead of practicing tomorrow, their bodies needed some rest, and their spirit needed to be refueled. It was time for connection.

Chapter 12

Commitment #5: Commit to Connect

The guys walked into the team meeting room sad and somber, with their heads down and their hearts and bodies aching. When they took their seats, Coach Richie shouted, "What is this, an undertaker's convention? Feels like we're at a freakin' funeral." He whistled and told them to get out of their seats and circle up. "Get in a circle and lock arms. This season isn't over. We've got a lot of games left. Remember our commitment to stay positive through challenges," he said as he stood in the middle of the circle and ran toward Teddy and Bussman, trying to break through their locked arms. They held tight and wouldn't budge. Then Coach ran toward Cons and Tim and couldn't break through their arms, either. Next he tried to run through Rock and H and once again he couldn't break through. He had them unlock their arms, and when they did he ran easily between them and made his way outside the circle.

"Too easy," he said as he walked back to the middle of the circle. "When you guys are connected, you are strong. When you are disconnected, you are weak. You guys are playing so hard and giving your best, but now it's time to give your best to each other."

Coach Richie pointed to their vision statement on the wall. "See that? It says, *One Gritty Team That Competes Like Champions*. You are definitely competing like champions individually. You are each being gritty in your play. But we are not being a gritty team together. You have individual grit but we don't have team grit because we are not *one* team. Team grit is all about connection. The more

73

connected we are, the more we become *one*. The more we become *one*, the more commitment, power, and grit we have *together*. You are all committed individually, but to be a great team you must be committed to each other, and that commitment is the result of connection. If you don't have connection, you will never have commitment. To be a committed team you must be a connected team. So as a team, we are going to commit to connect. That's our Fifth Commitment we must make as a team. It doesn't happen by accident. We have to be intentional and make time to connect. In this spirit, Coach Amy is now going to take you through a team building exercise to become more connected. We haven't done anything like this before, so give it a chance and let's see how it goes."

Coach Amy went to the board and wrote *One Word* on it. "I want each of you to choose a word for the rest of the season. A word that will motivate and inspire you. A word that will help you be your best. A word that will give you focus and purpose. What word will help you accomplish your goals? What word will help you keep your commitments? What word will help you and the team be our best? Take a few moments and think about it. There's no rush, so close your eyes and take your time to reflect. There's a word meant for you, and if you are open to it, I promise it will come to you and you'll see how it impacts you in a positive way the rest of the season."

Some of the guys closed their eyes, while some stared at the ceiling and others fiddled with their pens or fingers. One by one they wrote down their word and waited for their teammates to finish. After they all had their words, Coach Amy asked for a few volunteers to share what word they chose and why they chose it. "It's the *why* behind the word that gives it meaning and power. So I want to hear *why* you chose this word, since it's just as important—if not more important—than the word you chose. Does that make sense?" she asked.

The entire team responded, "Yes."

"Okay, wonderful. Who wants to go first?" she asked.

"I will," said Duff. "I chose *heart* because I want to put my heart and soul into this game and this team."

"I chose *drive*," said Hammer. "I'm allowing the losses to make me negative, and I know I need to drive us to be great." A bunch of the guys on the team rolled their eyes when Hammer said that.

"I choose *connect*," said Vino. I want to connect more with all you guys and do a better job of that."

"I like the word *overcome*," said Tim. "I feel like I have a lot to overcome, and I want us to overcome these losses so we can have a great rest of the season."

Joey sat there wanting to say something but told himself not to say it. He wasn't planning to share but something welled up deep inside of him, and he suddenly felt compelled to reveal his choice. "My word is *honor*. I already thought about this before the season, and I want to honor others with the way I play," he said with tears in his eyes.

"My word is *strong*," said Antonio. "I need to stay strong during this time, and we all need to stay strong for each other."

As each guy shared their word, the rest of the team clapped, and Amy wrote their word on the board. After each of the 34 guys had shared, Amy went to the board and read them all back to the team. Then she asked, "So what's going to be our team word? We need one word that will give our team focus and power going forward."

"How about *grit*?" said H.

"I like *connect*," said Rogers.

"I like *genesis*," said Bussman. "I feel like this is the beginning of something special, and I want this to be a new beginning for our team."

"I like the philosophy, Bussman. I don't know how you come up with half of the stuff you do but I really like it," replied Cons. "Yet I think our word is already chosen for us. I think this is the year of commitments, so our team word should be *commit*. What do you say?"

The team all agreed. It was the obvious and most fitting choice, and since Cons was so convincing, no one else even thought of another team word. And the truth was that in committing to connect via this exercise, they felt more connected as a team. Listening to each other's words and why they chose them helped them all understand what mattered most to one another and their thought process that drove their decisions.

Coach Amy gave each player and coach a rock to write their one word on it and encouraged them to keep their rock in the locker and look at it each day as a reminder to live the word. She even encouraged them to keep the rock in their pocket as they went to their classes. She also encouraged them to remind one another of their individual words and the team word in order to stay focused and committed. She wrote *Commit* on the board in huge letters.

The sting of yesterday's loss was replaced by a new word and, in Bussman's words, a new beginning. They were now looking forward, not backward. Coach Richie knew they weren't a fully connected team yet, but they had made progress and were on their way. He decided that they weren't going to practice tomorrow, either. One more day of drills wasn't going to make them a much better team, but the team building exercise he and Coach Amy planned would be far more valuable in the long run and could change everything.

Commitment #5: Commit to Connect

Chapter 13

The Safe Seat

Coach Amy placed a chair in the front of the room facing the rest of the team and called it the Safe Seat. She explained that it was a safe place to share and be honest, vulnerable, and transparent when participating in the next team building exercise, where they were going to share the 5 Hs. She wrote the 5 H questions on the board:

1. Who's your **Hero**?
2. What's a **Hardship** you faced that was a defining moment in your life?
3. What's a **Highlight** you are proud of?
4. What do you **Hope** for?
5. What's **Hilarious**? What makes you laugh? Could be a story or anything funny.

She had each guy sit in the Safe Seat one at a time and share their 5 Hs. A few guys got emotional talking about their heroes, who were often their father or grandfather. And they all laughed when guys talked about the hilarious pranks Coach Richie pulled on them, like telling Rogers to go ask the equipment guys for a bucket of steam for the locker room, or telling Duff to get phineoctopiene powder from the equipment guys, only to find out that there was no such thing as a bucket of steam or phineoctopiene powder. Many of the highlights focused on their wins together or the greatest moments in high school. When talking about their hopes, most of them expressed their desire to turn this season around and make the postseason playoffs. The most powerful moments happened when the players talked about their hardships, especially Tim, Joey, and Antonio.

Tim sat in the chair, nervous and shaking. He didn't want to say anything but something compelled him to start talking, and once he did, it all just came out. The story, the pain, the anger, and feeling like it was his fault. He cried as he shared that his father had left his mother, two brothers, and him when he was a boy. His mother was his hero for the way she responded and how she went to work and took care of him and his brothers. "She was my first and best coach and greatest encourager," he explained. "But my father, he was never there for me. He gave up on us. He was a quitter. I never want to be like that, and I never want to quit on the people I love. That's why I never want to quit on you guys. You are my team! I'm always going to keep fighting for you guys." He cried as he covered his eyes with his hands and put his head down. When he rose from the chair, a bunch of the guys got up to give him a hug before they all sat back down in their seats.

"Thank you for sharing, Tim," said Coach Amy. "I'm so proud of you for being vulnerable like that. You are making us all better by being you and being real and sharing your real hardship with us." She knew the ice had been broken and the soil was fertile. The moment was ripe and the rest of the guys were really going to share their hardship and feelings with the team. They felt safe to do so. To reinforce this safety, she reminded everyone, "Remember, this is a safe place. What is shared in this room stays in this room. You are a team and this is for your ears only."

After Tim she didn't have to call on anyone else to come sit in the Safe Seat. The guys just came forward ready and willing to be open and share their hearts.

Antonio sat in the Safe Seat and shared that his hardship was currently happening right now. His girlfriend had broken up with him and he was devastated. "There are times I think about ending it all so I don't have to feel this pain," he said with tears in his eyes. "She said she's still in love with her boyfriend from home. I thought that was over but clearly not. I thought she was the one. Now I don't know what to do. I feel lost and the only time I feel good is when I'm on the field playing with you guys. I feel like such a wimp for telling you all this, but I mean it when I say there are times I don't want to live. I know that sounds soft but it's true."

"It's not soft," said Rock. "It's honest and it means you're hurting. When my girlfriend broke up with me freshman year, I was depressed for a month but thankfully I got over it, and you guys, this team was a big part of me moving on. We got you, Antonio. No matter what you do, please don't give up. Don't do anything you will regret. You never know what God has for you. When you meet your wife you will be grateful this girlfriend broke up with you. As my dad says, fuggetttaboutit and move on to an even better future coming your way."

"I appreciate that," said Antonio. "I needed to hear that. Honestly, I feel better just sharing this with you all. I feel like it's not as big a deal as when I was just keeping it to myself."

"It's true," said Coach Amy. "It's why we're doing this. In isolation you become weak and powerless. Your negative thoughts and situations feel insurmountable. But when you connect with others, especially your team, you find a greater strength to get through tough times. We are stronger and better together. I'm proud of you for sharing this, Antonio, since I know so many of you have struggled or will struggle with this."

She pointed to Joey, who was shaking his head. "Let's finish the Safe Seat exercise with our last teammate to share." Joey didn't move. He couldn't. He didn't want to go. He felt like he would lose it if he did. But then he looked at Tim and Antonio. They were so raw and real. He couldn't believe they had shared what they did. He owed it to them to be real, too. He had never talked about it before with any of his teammates but today he would.

Joey sat in the seat and began crying before saying a word. He struggled to talk before breathing deeply a few times. And then, with his mouth quivering, he began pouring his heart out. He said his hero was his best friend and teammate in high school who died in a car crash after graduation, which was also his hardship. "We had just graduated and were talking about our plans to play in college. He was the best athlete and teammate I had ever been around. We talked about our hopes and dreams and couldn't believe they were coming true. We won a state championship and were going to play at the next level. Our only regret was that we weren't recruited and offered a scholarship by the same school, so we wouldn't be playing together in college. But man, we were so happy for each other. But then one night while coming back from his girlfriend's house, his car got hit by a driver running a red light, and just like that he was gone. The dreams, the plans, the future, my best friend gone just like that. I miss him so much. His number was 11, and it's why I wear number 11. I play to honor him and give my all to achieve the goals we both set for ourselves. I can't let him down. I won't let him down. But man, I wish he was still here. He was my brother, and I think about him all the time."

The guys were stunned. They had no idea. But Coach Richie and his staff knew what had happened. They had talked with Joey a bunch of times since he had been at college, helping him deal with his sadness and at times depression. Joey had never shared this with the team before, and as a sophomore it felt like a huge relief to get it all out. And the team now understood why Joey was adamant about wearing number 11 ever since he joined the team and why he wrote number 11 on the palm of his hand before every game.

Joey got up from the chair with tears streaming down his face, and his teammates approached him and hugged him. When Cons hugged him, he said loud enough for the entire team to hear, "We are your brothers now. We got you. We can't replace him but we can be your teammates like him." The entire team nodded as they spontaneously formed a circle around him and hugged him and each other.

The Safe Seat

Chapter 14

Team Beats Talent

Coach Amy had never seen the 5 Hs go wrong. Every team she had ever shared it with became more connected, and this time and this team was no different. They walked into the room as disconnected individuals and walked out a connected team. In sharing themselves and their stories, a special spirit filled the room. The walls of pride, envy, and ego came crumbling down, and what was left was always there. It was love. Love is often surrounded by fear, cluttered by negative thoughts, guilt, and shame, and covered by our past and pain. Yet when you remove all that stuff and get rid of your pride and ego and get to the truth in your heart, love is all that remains. This love creates a feeling of oneness and connection. It's why love drives grit and commitment. When you love something, you don't quit on it. When you love someone, you don't quit on them. You have a connection to what you do and to the team you do it with. When you love someone and are connected to them, you will fight for them. When adversity strikes, instead of running away from each other, you run toward each other. Coach Richie and Coach Amy knew this team was never going to be the same. They were more concerned about developing them as people and leaders off the field, but were also excited to see how their love, connection, and team grit would show up on the field.

In the weeks that followed, Coach Richie watched as this team became the most connected team he had ever coached. He had seen too many teams in the past be derailed by jealousy, bitterness, divisiveness, and cliques, but Coach Amy's exercises proved to be a potent antidote to those ailments. They weren't the most talented team he had ever coached, but the love they had for each other and the connection they had in the locker room and on the field was like nothing he and his staff had ever seen, and it transformed them into a real and special team. They went on a four-game winning streak, beating several teams that were more talented, but because they were the more connected team, they won. He told his team, "Team beats talent when talent isn't a team. So let's keep getting better and developing our talent and keep playing as one." They were 9–4, and a few more wins would give them a chance to make the postseason.

They won the next game, improving their record to 10–4, but then lost the next two because even though they were deeply connected, there were still a few guys being selfish, a few guys making mistakes at the worst possible time, and truthfully one of the opposing teams was more talented and played better that game. Coach knew that just because you were connected didn't mean you would win, but it did give you a much better chance of winning. He also knew they had to address the selfishness and hero ball some of the guys were displaying and have a difficult conversation about what was holding them back from being their best. With a record of 10–6, if they wanted to finish strong and make the postseason, they needed more than a greater connection to each other. They needed a few more wins and a greater commitment to each other.

Chapter 15

Commitment #6: Commit to Each Other

As the players took their seats in the meeting room, Coach Amy smiled and said, "Okay, it's time for some difficult conversations. I hope you're ready for this exercise because it's going to be a good one. Challenging but good." She handed out plain white paper with each person's name at the top on one side and sticky tape on the other side. She instructed the players to stick the paper on each other's backs so everyone had a sheet of paper on their back. She had them all come to the open space in the front of the room and asked seven teammates to stand side by side while she handed out markers to the rest of them.

"Now, on the white paper on your teammates' backs, write a few words that represent what you believe is holding that teammate back from being their best and being a great teammate. After we've done the first seven, the next seven will line up and you'll write on their backs. When we're all done, we're going to have some difficult conversations."

Coach Richie watched as the guys looked at each other. He knew they were asking themselves how honest they should be. Should they really say it? Should they write it? Thinking it is one thing but once you say it and write it there's no turning back. "I want you all to be honest. This is the part where we challenge each other like we discussed in the past," he said in a raised voice. "This is the part where we make each other better. If you don't say it, you won't be helping your teammates grow. If you stay quiet, things will stay the same, and the same isn't good enough for a committed team that wants to be great. This

Commitment #6: Commit to Each Other

is your time to say what needs to be said, so let's all say it because we need to hear it. We got some elephants in this room, and it's time to address the elephants and make them disappear."

The guys were pensive, thinking about what they should write, but once they started there was no stopping them. When they were finished with the first seven team-mates, the next seven lined up, until every player had a list of words of what was keeping them from being their best and being a great teammate.

When they were done Coach Amy wrote on the board:

Commitment #6: Commit to Each Other

- You must commit to serve and sacrifice for each other.
- What will you do to be a great teammate?
- How will you sacrifice for your team?
- What will you give up?
- What will you give?

She then had one guy at a time come to the front of the room and take the paper off their back, sit in the Safe Seat, and read out loud what was written on the paper. After the reading, she asked them what they thought about it and how it made them feel.

Duff read the words "Focus," "Work harder," and "Cocky" and said he understood the cocky part because he plays with a chip on his shoulder. "I have to because I'm a freshman, and I need to tell myself I belong. But I don't get the focus and work harder part."

"As a freshman you don't work as hard as you need to, to get better," said Tills. "This is another level, and your practice habits and focus are still at the high school level. You need to race to maturity."

"And when it comes to being cocky, I like your confidence," Cons said as he pointed to Duff. "But sometimes you come across like you are so confident you only care about yourself and don't care about anyone else. It sometimes feels like arrogance. That disconnects you from your teammates. You need to work on that."

"How does that make you feel?" asked Coach Amy.

"I never saw myself like that," said Duff. "But if that's what my teammates think, I'm definitely going to work on it. I'll work on my focus and my practice habits. I'm not going to lose my confidence, though. I need that. I'm not letting go of that."

"No one wants you to lose that," exclaimed Coach Richie. "That's why I brought you here. Just make sure it's the confidence that makes you and your team better, and not the cockiness that makes only you feel better."

As Teddy sat in the chair he read the words "Discipline," "Devotion," "Be more serious," and "Distractions." He agreed 100 percent with what was written and knew he needed to give more to the team to be his best and make the team better. He loved to have fun and sometimes had too much fun and needed to tune out the distractions

95

during the year. He vowed to give up the distractions and said he was going to give his all to the team. He was going to be a great teammate by sacrificing the things he wanted to do, in order to do the things he must do to make the team the best it could be.

For Rogers there was only one big word on his sheet of paper that everyone agreed with, and no one had to add anything: "Listen." When asked how it made him feel, he said he had no clue why it was written.

"Because you don't listen," said Hammer. "And you definitely don't hear."

Rogers was going to yell back at Hammer but Vino interjected before he could do so. "When Coach tells you to do something you nod your head, but then you do what you want to do," said Vino. We need you to listen, especially in the last few minutes of games where we're making some mistakes that are hurting us."

"I'm just in the moment. I'm amped up. It's hard for me to listen," said Rogers. "I see the mouth moving but I'm thinking about what I need to do next."

"That's great to know," said Coach Richie. "From now on I'm going to ask you to repeat back to me what I said to make sure we're all on the same page. I think we just solved a big problem with this exercise. It's not that you don't want to listen. You're just having trouble listening. So you commit to work on your listening and I'll commit to making sure you heard what I said. Oh, baby!"

Tim didn't like reading the words on his paper: "Inconsistent under pressure," "Weak in practice," "Checks out sometimes." He didn't know what to say when Coach Amy asked him how it made him feel. He paused for a few seconds. "It doesn't feel good," he said. "I never thought about it but now that I'm reading it, I can see what they mean. I've always been a gamer. Was never good in practice."

"But you've got to bring more to practice to make the team better. Can you do that?" asked Tills.

"I can. I will work on that," said Tim. "And I know what you mean about being inconsistent under pressure. Sometimes when the game is on the line I want the ball to come my way. I've often risen to the occasion in the past. I've made the big play often. But truthfully there are times I don't want to fail and don't want to let you guys down and that's why I check out. So I can see why you guys would say that. I needed to hear that."

Coach Amy interjected. "It's because your identity is tied to your performance, Tim. If you succeed, you are worthy and your existence matters. You validate yourself through your successes. This is a safe place so I can tell you it's likely because your father left when you were young and because you felt invalidated, you have spent your life and playing career validating yourself through your accomplishments. In the moments when you're afraid to fail you believe that if you fail, you are a failure. If you don't succeed, then you are worth nothing. So you check out to avoid a possible failure and, even worse, the horrible feeling that comes from that. The answer is not to tie your identity to your performance and the outcome. We love and support you no matter what! Don't we, guys!?"

Commitment #6: Commit to Each Other

"Yes," they all yelled.

"We got you, Tim!" shouted Cons.

"So what will you give and give up?" asked Coach Amy.

"I'm going to give up worrying about the outcome. It's exhausting," said Tim. "I'm going to give up my fear of failure. I'm going to give more in practice to make my team better. And I'm going to give my all in big moments and not check out. I just need to go for it and not let the outcome define me."

"I love hearing that, and we will be here to help you. This is going really great. We are definitely getting better from this," said Coach Amy as she motioned for Hammer to go sit in the Safe Seat. She had a feeling this one was going to be the most challenging of all, and she was right. Hammer took his seat and read the words "Not a leader," "Attitude," and "Selfish." He shook his head, not knowing what to say. He was embarrassed. "It's not true. I'm not selfish. I'm always trying to get you guys to do what we need to do," he said. "When you're slacking, I'm the only leader who says something."

"What do you mean, it's not true?" exclaimed Rogers. "It's very true. You think you're a leader but you aren't. Telling someone what to do doesn't make you a leader."

"Your attitude gets in the way of your leadership," said Tills. I know you care but it's often at the expense of making your teammates feel like crap."

"There's no encouragement from you whatsoever. Always nagging," said Bussman.

"You're selfish on the field," said Cons. "You try to do it all yourself because you don't trust your teammates and this makes you a bad leader, too. You're telling everyone what to do but really it's all about you."

"We love you, Hammer, but it's true," said H. "We all see it but the fact you don't says everything."

"So what are you going to do about it?" asked Vino.

"I don't know what to do," said Hammer, who was shocked that his teammates thought this way about him. He always believed he was a great leader. He clearly saw himself much differently than everyone saw him. He felt like he was being attacked with wrecking balls as the core of who he thought he was crumbled. "I have a lot to think about. But if you guys say I have a negative attitude, then I have to give that up. I also need to give up telling everyone what to do and focus on becoming a better leader. So, yeah, I'm going to think about how I can be a better teammate and be a more positive leader. If my attitude and leadership are holding us back, then I have to change."

"It's for your own good and the good of our team," said Coach Richie. "You boys have a lot to think about as we get ready for our final stretch and last few games of the season. Before you leave today, I want you to think about one way you are going to be a great teammate the rest of the season and write it up here on the board. If we do that and commit to each other, I know we're going to finish strong and head into the postseason stronger than ever."

That night, as each teammate lay in their beds thinking about what they needed to do to sacrifice for the team and be a great teammate, Hammer thought about what his teammates said about him. He was hurting and angry. How could he be so misunderstood? "I care more about them than they care about me. I don't even want to play the last few games. Let's see how they do without me," he thought.

In that moment he heard his own selfishness, negativity, and poor leadership. They were right. He was more focused on himself than on the team. He told people what to do so they would play better so he could win. He cared more about winning than how his teammates felt. He cared about how he played more than if the team won. He wasn't the leader he thought he was, but he vowed he would start working on being the leader they needed him to be. It was a defining moment in his life, and he and his team would be forever transformed by this exercise and their own willingness to change, improve, sacrifice, and become better teammates.

With a few games left and a few wins needed to make the postseason, Coach Richie hoped their transformation would also transform their play on the field.

Chapter 16

LOSS

Coach Richie reminded his team once again that a season is like a roller coaster. With more ups and downs than ever this year, he and his staff were not surprised that they won their next game and lost the game after that. The win was special because they played so well together. They finally jelled on the field and played connected, committed, and as one. The loss was devastating because they were once again playing so well together until H went down with a severe knee injury that required a cart to take him off the field. The guys gathered around him and were visibly shaken by seeing a teammate they had grown to love and care for lying on the field with his body facing in one direction and his leg in another direction. They knew his season and maybe even his playing career was done, and seeing him in such agony was traumatic and painful. Coach Richie had tears in his eyes, and while he wished his team could forget about it and move on, when play resumed they weren't the same team. They lost the lead in the fourth quarter and never recovered.

The next day as the team stood in a circle on the practice field, Coach Richie declared, "Murphy's Law says that bad things will happen at the worst possible time. Well, it happened to us and, guess what, I hate Murphy. I think of Murphy as a guy who shows up and wants to ruin your season and your career. Well, I say when Murphy shows up, we beat Murphy. We don't let him beat us. Instead of worrying about Murphy with a victim mindset, let's expect him to show up and know that we are stronger and tougher than Murphy. We won't let him beat us. We will beat him. Are you with me?"

"Yes, Coach!" they all shouted.

"Now I know you care about H, and I know it's very normal that the way he got hurt affected us. I bet if you didn't care about him like a brother, you wouldn't have been affected. You would have just kept playing your game, focusing on yourself. But the fact that you guys kept thinking about him told me that you truly care about him and about each other. We lost our focus and we lost the game. I'm not mad at all. *LOSS* stands for Learning Opportunity, Stay Strong, so I want us to take the lesson from this loss, and stay strong as we approach our last game of the regular season. If we win, we get to spend more time together for a postseason run. If we lose, our season is over. It's win or go home, boys. What do you want to do?"

"*Win!*" everyone shouted.

"That's great," responded Coach Richie. "Then let's do it together as one. When adversity strikes and a big challenge comes our way again, which it surely will, let's learn from this partner in growth called Murphy and band together and overcome together. Oh, baby, it's great to be here."

Chapter 17

I Am...

The next day at practice, a day before their final game, Coach Amy stood in the middle of the circle and looked at the team, including H, who was on crutches and awaiting surgery. His knee was too swollen to have surgery yet, and he loved his team too much not to be with them before the big game. "You are not the thoughts you think. You are the thoughts you believe," said Coach Amy. "As a man thinks, he becomes. The thoughts you think and the words you say become the life you create. So think about what would happen if you said, 'I am strong. I am powerful. I am a champion.' I want each of you to come into the circle one at a time and say, 'I am' and then add another word. Speak life into who you are. Say it and become it!"

The guys looked at each other. They felt awkward at first, but they were used to feeling awkward this season. And like so many of the exercises they did this season, their discomfort turned into transformation.

"I am confident," said Duff.

"I am a warrior!" shouted Rogers.

"I am a champion!" shouted Tills.

"I am powerful!" shouted Vino.

"I am a great teammate," said Hammer in a way that let his team know he was working on it.

"I am enough," said Antonio.

It was truly powerful, but even more powerful was when Cons went back into the middle of the circle after they all shared their "I am" statements, and said, "Listen, boys. H can no longer play with us but we can play for him. He's demonstrated his commitment to being with us even after his injury. Most guys wouldn't be here, but he is. So let's commit to giving our best for him."

"I appreciate that, Cons," said H with tears in his eyes. "Let's win this one for each other. You are my brothers and I love you guys."

Cons said, "Okay, boys, when I yell, 'I am,' I want you all to you yell, 'My brother's keeper!'"

Cons yelled, "I am!"

And the team shouted back, "My brother's keeper!"

He yelled again, "I am!"

Again they shouted, 'My brother's keeper!'"

They were a team ready to play and ready to win.

Chapter 18

Stronger Together

The team showed up to the game field with the number 11 written on their hands. If it was important to Joey, it was important to them. When Joey saw this he no longer played just for his high school teammate. He now played for all his teammates as well, and they played for him. When they got to their sideline they placed their One Word rocks on the bench and warmed up with an unprecedented focus and determination. This team wasn't worried about losing. They were focused on their commitments and competing and preparing to win. They didn't want their season to end and because they played with confidence, determination, unity, and selflessness, it didn't. They played their best game of the season and left no doubt who was the better team. They did it. They had made it to the postseason, and when they got to the locker room they danced like they had never danced before.

"I'm proud of you guys," said Coach Richie. "Not because you won. I'm proud of you because of the team you have become. You've done everything we've asked, and this is the reward of being humble and willing and dedicated to growth. When you honor your commitments and pay the price that greatness requires, your commitments will pay you back. And guess what—we are not done growing, so let's keep committing to each other and see what we can do and how high we can rise. Let's get ready for a quick turnaround since the postseason starts in two days. Make sure you ice those legs, eat healthy food, and get ready to compete like champions. It's great to be here."

Chapter 19

An Unexpected Fan

The team peaked at the right time, competed like champions, and won the next three postseason games, making it to the quarterfinals. They received a ton of press and accolades from the media and their fans. Several of their plays even made it on SportsCenter, and they had garnered national attention. Yet they had learned their lesson of the past not to believe the hype. Coach Richie reminded them they were one overconfident game away from being eliminated from the postseason: "We don't win games in the media. We win on the field. Focus on what you are here to do and not on what they say about you."

While the guys were doing their best to ignore what the media was saying, their families and friends were reading and watching everything. Including estranged family members like Tim's father. Tim hadn't seen or talked to him in years but he reached out to Tim and said he was coming to see him play in the quarterfinals game. Tim was a wreck leading up to the game. His teammates didn't know what was going on but they knew something was wrong. During a team building session two days before the quarterfinals, Coach Amy asked the guys to share anything they were struggling with. Tim told the team about his father calling him and coming to the game.

"How do you feel about that?" asked Coach Amy.

"It's making me a wreck," said Tim. "I mean, the guy is absent for years and because now I'm on TV and part of this team he wants to come back into my life and screw this up for me. He's done enough to screw my life up. I don't need this. I don't get it. What gives?"

An Unexpected Fan

"You can tell him not to come," said Hammer, trying to be more supportive.

"I could. But it's a free country. If he wants to come he can come," said Tim. "I just can't let it bother me so much."

"I'm just glad you told us," said Tills. "If you didn't, we wouldn't know what was wrong with you and we'd be going into this game disconnected. But now that we know we can support you."

"Yeah, we got you," said Vino. "We are your family. We got you!"

"I appreciate that," said Tim. "Knowing you guys have my back means the world. I feel better about this. I'm just going to play inside out and do my thing, and I'll see him after the game and see how it goes."

"That's a great idea," said Coach Amy, who knew that if it wasn't for these team building sessions they wouldn't have been connected enough for Tim to share something like this. But because they felt safe to be vulnerable, Tim could share what was making him feel weak so his team could provide a collective strength.

The team played the quarterfinal game with a collective strength that overpowered their opponent and won by several goals. Hammer led in a positive and encouraging way. Rogers listened much better than usual. Antonio was more focused on the game than on his girlfriend. Duff played with confidence and not cockiness, and Tim played his best game of the year and rose to the occasion during the biggest moments of the game. The team was overjoyed that they were heading to the Final Four and a chance to win a national championship.

After the game Tim walked over to the stands to see his father, who had made his way onto the field. He looked much older than Tim remembered and was visibly nervous. They shared an awkward exchange and small talk. Tim wasn't in the mood to hug him or get into details of their past. But when his father said it was great to watch him play and that he was proud of him, Tim began to cry, gave him a hug, thanked him for coming, and said he had to go celebrate with the team.

Tim had questions and wanted answers, but that would have to be another conversation for another day. This wasn't the time or the place to get into it. Besides, it was time to go dance with his team. When Tim turned around to head back to the locker room, he was surprised to see his entire team standing behind him. And as they walked to the locker room, they put their arms around him and celebrated their big win!

Chapter 20

Forever Teammates

The team won their semifinal game in a jam-packed stadium against a really great team. They were losing by three goals when Coach Richie called a timeout and exclaimed, "Oh, baby, it's great to be here. These are the moments we live for. Right now, turn your frustration into focus and any fear you have into fuel. Love the battle. Love competing. Love each other. I love and believe in you guys."

The team responded with a fierce positive focus. Through relentless determination and incredible teamwork, they came back to win the game. Coach Richie said a team that stays positive together and stays committed together achieves uncommon results, and this team was certainly doing uncommon things to achieve uncommon victories. No one expected this kind of a season from this team, but when you become a committed team you expect to win and go beyond the expectation of others.

Two days later the team walked into the stadium to play in the national championship expecting to win, and they played their best game of the season and competed like champions, but on this day they didn't win a championship. They gave their all and played beautifully together but their opponent was the better, more talented team who were also connected and committed.

As the guys sat in the locker room with their heads down, Coach Richie walked in, whistled, and shouted, "Keep your heads up, men! Losers put their heads down and you aren't losers. You didn't win today but that doesn't make you losers. I couldn't be more proud of the way you played. Your heart and effort and will and skill were on display for the world to see, and you made yourself proud, you made us proud, you made your families proud, and you made this university and your fans proud. They were just better than us today. That's going to happen. Being a committed team doesn't mean you are always going to win a championship. But it does mean you will compete like champions, and that's what you boys did. You lived the vision and mission we set forth in the beginning of the year. You became One Gritty Team That Competed Like Champions, and you set the standard for every team that will come after you. This team right here will inspire future teams to be great! Do you hear what I'm saying?"

"Yes, Coach!" they all shouted .

"Trophies don't last," he continued. "They break. They get lost. They get thrown out. They lose their significance. In a few hundred years no one will care about whether you won a championship trophy. But the way you cared about each other and loved each other and played for each other, that's what lasts forever. It's the love that lasts forever, and that's why you all are forever teammates!"

Chapter 21

The 6 Commitments

Tim and Vino sat on the balcony of Vino's office, which felt like a million miles and a million years from where and when they played that national championship game.

"Do you wish we had won?" asked Vino.

"Of course," answered Tim. "But then I wonder if we would be the same if we did. Sometimes you wish you could go back and change things, and I have this theory that if you could have a do-over and change the outcome, you wouldn't like how your life turned out. So while I wish we had won, I wouldn't change a thing. Who knows if we would have had a moment like this if we had won. You just don't know."

"I know what you mean. I don't think I would have worked as hard or made relationships such a big priority like I've done in my career if we had won. I think it made me appreciate people more than trophies. But I sure would have liked to have that trophy," Vino said, laughing as he slapped Tim on the back.

"I want to thank you for making time for me today. I needed this. I forgot so many things you helped me remember, and I know this is going to help me and my company going forward," Tim said as he got up and gave his old teammate a big hug.

"You got it, pal. Nothing I love more than getting together with my friends and remembering our past to help create a great future. And I have a feeling we'll be seeing each other sooner rather than later under unfortunate circumstances. I'm going to go see Coach Richie before that day. In the meantime, just make sure you use these 6 Commitments," said Vino as he pulled out a sheet of paper from his notebook with the 6 Commitments written on it and handed it to Tim.

"Thank you," said Tim as he walked out the door and toward the elevator that took him to the parking garage. As he drove away from Vino's building, he glanced at the sheet of paper on the front passenger seat. "If these 6 Commitments could help a ragtag bunch of knuckleheads like us make it to a national championship," he thought, "I can only imagine what they can do for my team at work. I just have to decide how to introduce them to my team." He had wanted to ask Vino how he introduced them to his own team and company but hadn't wanted to take up any more of his time. Besides, he was a little emotional remembering some of the best yet most painful moments of his life.

Tim thought about what he was like back then and how those times with his team and Coach Richie's fatherly influence transformed him as a man and leader. And he smiled thinking about how Coach Richie and his teammates like Vino were still impacting him now, years later. His father had passed away a few years after he graduated college. Although they eventually developed a cordial relationship, it lacked the depth and connection that only comes from spending time together when you're growing up. Tim leaned on his family and teammates who became his brothers for advice, friendship, and support. And with Vino reminding him of the 6 Commitments, they were helping him once again.

As he drove on, Coach Amy popped into Tim's head. He remembered seeing her 10 years earlier at an alumni event, where she told him about workshops she did helping teams implement the 6 Commitments. At the time he and his company were growing exponentially and the last thing he was thinking about was leadership, culture, and teamwork. He was too busy trying to fly the rocket ship and make sure it didn't crash. He brushed it off at the time, but somehow this memory came back to him and he now wondered if she was still doing them. She would be in her 60s now and maybe she had retired.

He pulled over and took out his phone to google Coach Amy. Right there on the screen was Coach Amy and the 6 Commitments. He opened the contacts on his phone, found her cell number, and called her. She picked up right away. They talked about Coach Richie and his visit with Vino. He explained his situation at work. She told him how she had been doing these workshops for years. She had heard that Vino had implemented the 6 Commitments on his own but knew that many leaders needed help with the process, and that's where she came in.

"Well, I'm one of those leaders who needs help," said Tim, and they agreed to have her fly in to do a workshop with his leadership team the next week. Coach Amy encouraged him to do a full-day workshop with his leadership team first and go through all 6 Commitments and interactive exercises with them, before rolling out one commitment a month to the entire company virtually. As she explained, a team that's not connected at the top will crumble at the bottom. The goal was to get the leadership team aligned and committed, and once that happened they would be in a great position to get everyone in the company united and committed.

Tim loved the plan. He had already experienced the impact the 6 Commitments had on his college team. If they had even half the impact on his company, he would be very happy.

Chapter 22

Commitment Recognizes Commitment

Going through the 6 Commitments with his team and Coach Amy was like being in a time machine. With each commitment he reflected on the past and saw how it applied to his present team and situation. He and his team engaged in great discussions and also had several difficult conversations where the truth came out, that he wasn't always a committed leader. At the beginning of the workshop, Tim thought his team was the problem. By the end it was apparent that he needed to be a better leader. He needed to be more committed to them if he wanted them to be committed.

"Commitment recognizes commitment," said Coach Amy. "The more you commit, the more it will come back to you." Tim marveled at how Coach Amy had mastered the commitments and was prepared for every issue and nuance that came up during her teaching, as she helped guide the decisions of how each person and the team would implement the commitments. The fact that Tim took ownership of his lack of commitment helped greatly, and his vulnerability helped the team become vulnerable. They saw that as the leader, he wanted to improve and it made them want to improve. Tim realized it all started with him. It always starts with the leader. Coach Richie had led the way, and that changed everything. Tim would need to become more like him to change everything for his team and his company.

The 5 Hs exercise was a game-changer for his team, just like it was for his college team. It helped him learn things about his colleagues that he didn't know, despite

Commitment Recognizes Commitment

working with some of them for over 12 years. He clearly had more work to do to put Commitments #5 and #6 into practice and connect with and commit to his team. Coach Richie did that for him all these years, and he needed to do it for them.

He was thinking about Coach Richie and how he would commit more when he got the call that Coach Richie had passed away and the funeral was set for Monday.

Chapter 23

The Funeral

Tim thought he had cried his last tear after telling his family that Coach Richie had passed away. But as soon as he saw his teammates, the tears started flowing once again. He hadn't seen many of them in a long time. Some he hadn't seen since they graduated. Life flies by when you begin your career, meet your spouse, have kids, start and grow a business, and raise a family.

In seeing his teammates, Tim felt the converging of time as his past and present merged into one moment. The memories he had with his teammates felt like a lifetime ago, and yet because their bond was so strong and their common experiences were so familiar, it felt like he had seen them yesterday. In connecting and talking with each of his teammates, 30 years felt like 30 minutes. Time had flown by and yet it went back to the past even faster. He was looking at the older version of them and seeing the younger version at the same time. Some guys looked like they could still play. Others looked like they needed to lay off the desserts and start walking each day. Some guys still had hair, while others shaved what they had left.

It was the saddest of times saying goodbye to Coach Richie, and yet it was energizing to connect with his old friends and teammates and see guys who played years before and after he did. They were like one huge family, and Coach Richie was a father to all of them. It was truly special when the guys who won a national championship after Tim graduated came up to him and his teammates and thanked them for being the program that changed everything. They credited them with setting the

The Funeral

standard that inspired them to win it all. "Without you, we wouldn't have won a championship," they said as they showed off their rings.

"Well, I'm glad we could help you get that hardware," Tim said, laughing, wishing he had a ring but still feeling proud that he and his team had helped make it possible.

During the service, Tim looked around the room and saw hundreds of players Coach Richie had coached over the years, including many of his staff. He sat near his teammates Duff, Cons, Teddy, Bussman, Tills, Vino, Rock, Rogers, H, Joey, Hammer, Antonio, and all the other members of his team who were able to make it. He had texted them all to say that if they were coming, they should bring their One Word rock. He had an idea.

While Monseigneur Mark talked about the impact Coach Richie had on so many, Tim looked at all the faces and thought about all the lives he touched. No one really had to talk about his legacy. His legacy was in this room for all to see. They were boys who would become better men, husbands, fathers, and leaders because Coach Richie truly cared about them. Billy Graham said a coach will impact more people in a year than the average person does in a lifetime, and that was true for Coach Richie.

Tim asked himself whether you had to be a coach to make an impact like that, and he decided in that moment that you didn't have to be an actual coach. You just had to care like a coach, and coach others to make a difference. That's the kind of leader and coach he wanted to be going forward. The way Coach Richie did it in the locker room, he could do it in the office and the conference room. Monseigneur Mark said Coach Richie didn't just impact your life; he put his fingerprint on your soul, and Tim decided he wanted to put his fingerprint on the souls of those he led. If it wasn't for Coach Richie, he wouldn't be the person he had become, and Tim wanted others to be able to say the same about his leadership.

After the service they drove to the burial site. When they were finished lowering the casket into the ground, Tim and his teammates took their One Word rocks from their pockets and put them in the burial container on top of the flat casket. Coach Richie said teammates are forever, and so are coaches who change your life.

As Tim drove to the airport to head home, he asked himself once again, "Are teammates forever? Are coaches forever? Even though they put the One Word rocks into the casket to symbolize their unity and commitment forever, is it really forever? After all, the body turns to dust and eventually so will the rocks. And then it hit Tim. He saw it so clearly. Everything in life is temporary. Nothing physical lasts forever. Appearance is temporary. But essence is eternal. As Coach Richie said, it's the love that lasts. It's the care you put into what you do, and the people you do it with, that lasts forever and ripples into eternity. Every moment is an eternal moment to make an eternal impact. Being a forever teammate and a forever coach is not about trophies. It's about putting your heart and soul, love and care into everything you do.

The Funeral

Tim thought about Coach Richie. He thought about his own mortality and the fact that one day we will all be gone. And when that day comes, all that will remain is the love and care we put into every moment, every practice, every game, every team building session, every interaction, every relationship. It's what made his team so special and so great. It was the relationships, the connection, the feeling of oneness, the pursuit of something challenging, the commitments, and the mission they had together that made them forever teammates. Tim made an adjustment in his mind to Coach Richie's saying. He decided that teammates actually are not forever. It's the teammates who love and care about each other and commit to each other that are forever. And a coach who loves and cares about you and puts their fingerprint on your soul is a forever coach. From now on he wanted to be a forever coach and a forever teammate.

Chapter 24

The Power Inside You

A few weeks later, Tim shared his thoughts and ideas with Coach Amy. He wanted his employees to become forever teammates, and he wanted to provide practical tips to create something tangible when dealing with such an ethereal idea as "forever." He made a video and shared it with everyone in the company, talking about the power of caring and creating your life and success from the inside out. He told them that being a forever teammate is possible in every moment by reminding yourself, "This matters. This meeting matters. What I'm doing matters. This person matters. This mission matters. This team matters. This effort matters. This client matters. If it matters to you and you care about it, you will put this care into the person, the project, the meeting, the team, and the client. And the care you put into it will determine the quality of it."

Coach Amy recommended that Tim bring in Damon West as a keynote speaker, who talked about the coffee bean as a great analogy and a lesson to empower all his employees with the idea that they have the power inside them to transform their culture, company, team, and relationships from the inside out. Damon came to speak and gave a great talk that inspired everyone to live and create inside out.

In Tim's office after the speech, he told Damon he loved his speech but shared that he was trying to figure out how to get all his employees to understand how to create a collective power within the team. He loved the exercises he did with Coach Richie and Coach Amy, but he felt like there was something missing. He asked Damon what was the most powerful team building exercise he had ever done.

Damon replied, "I can't tell you the most powerful exercise I've ever done because I don't do team building exercises, but I can tell you the most powerful team building exercise I've ever witnessed. I was in prison, which as I told in my story to your people today is where I learned the coffee bean lesson. Definitely not proud of my past, but proud of what I've learned and who I've become and all the people I help now. So anyway, I'm in our large meeting room in prison, and a bunch of prisoners are sitting in a row of chairs. They have no idea what's coming next, so there is some tension in the room. Then in walks a bunch of men of all ages from the free world with towels and buckets of water, and they proceed to wash the prisoners' feet. Now let me tell you, touching a man's feet in prison is cause for a big fight. The prisoners didn't know what to do at first. Usually the only physical touch in a prison is violence. But in just a few minutes that tension transformed into tears. As music played, these tough, hardened criminals cried like babies. When the free men were done washing their feet, the prisoners asked if they could return the favor. No one in that room was ever the same after that."

Tim knew he wasn't about to have his employees wash each other's feet. He joked that there must be some HR policy that says you can't do it, but he did realize why the exercise was so powerful and why it made a difference. The prisoners felt valued. For some it might have been the first time in their entire life that someone valued them. And when you are in prison you lose any value you had. Prisoners aren't considered valuable. Yet here were these free men making them feel valued, which changed how they saw themselves. It felt so positive that they wanted to return that feeling by valuing the men who showed up to value them. This was the missing piece Tim had been looking for. There was a missing 7th Commitment, and Tim knew exactly what it was.

Chapter 25

The 7th Commitment

After Damon left, Tim and Amy continued the conversation about the 7th Commitment. Coach Amy had been teaching the 6 Commitments so long it felt strange to hear there was a 7th Commitment but she was open to getting better. Tim went to the board and wrote:

The 7th Commitment: Commit to Valuing Each Other

Tim explained, "If you don't value each other and find value in your team members, then none of the other commitments work or make sense. You first have to value each other and value the team. If you do, you'll commit to giving your all to the team and commit to getting better together and commit to connecting with each other and commit to sacrificing for each other. If you value your team, you'll do all of it. But if you don't value each other, you won't do any of it."

So while this was the 7th Commitment, Tim thought it really should be the 1st Commitment and the first one taught to a team. Tim wrote down in his notebook: *The last shall be first and the first shall be last.*

Tim wondered how he would put this into practice and help his team implement it. He and Coach Amy brainstormed ideas and came up with VALUE. He and his leadership team would focus on valuing their employees and making them feel valued and show them what it looks like to VALUE each other. He knew that some people felt like their job was a prison sentence they had to endure, and hopefully if they felt valued like those prisoners did, he could liberate them. "If it worked in a prison, surely it could work in an office," he said, laughing.

Tim wrote on the whiteboard in his office:

V-alidate

A-ppreciate

L-isten

U-nderstand

E-mpathize

He and his team would make each other and everyone in the organization feel validated and feel like the work they were doing mattered. They would appreciate each other for who they are and what they do. They would truly take the time and energy to listen to and understand each other, even if they disagreed. This would go a long way in having difficult conversations that ultimately made them better. And they would have empathy when dealing with each other and try to put themselves in each other's shoes, see things from their perspective and feel their emotions. This is what happened with Coach Richie and their team, and it didn't happen by accident. It happened because they focused on it and did team building sessions that created connection that led to empathy and understanding and valuing each other even more.

Tim decided that in addition to having his leaders do team building exercises with their teams, he was going to do a weekly video for the entire company, and he would also start sharing selfie videos with a direct personal message to several employees each day. The first one he did was to Julie, the head of product development, where he recorded himself saying, "Hey, Julie, just want to thank you for all your hard work. What you did for our recent product launch was amazing, and I appreciate you working long hours to get it done. We couldn't have done it without you." Then he shared another video with Marlo, a customer service supervisor, saying, "Marlo you are awesome. You are always on top of everything. When that customer needed support, you jumped in right a way and took care of it. Thanks for being so attentive and focused and responsive. You care so much and it shows. Thank you and keep up the great work." Both of them responded immediately, saying how grateful they were to receive his video and message. Tim could tell that his genuine, specific praise—not the generic "good job" he used to say—truly resonated and was going to be a game-changer going forward. His team and company were already feeling and acting differently, and he was excited about going to the next level. Thanks to Coach Amy and the 7 Commitments, he was more confident and committed than ever.

Chapter 26

Forever Impact

It had been a month since Coach Richie's funeral. Tim and his teammates created a group text thread after the funeral, and on this day his phone was blowing up with messages.

```
Did you get it?
Did you get it?
I got it!
I got it!
```

Got what? Tim responded.

```
Just check your mailbox when you get
home from work, H texted back.
```

When he got home he went straight to the mailbox and found a box that said it was from Coach Richie. "This is weird," he thought as he opened the box to find a smaller box and a card inside. He opened it and saw a handwritten note from Coach Richie:

Hey kid, when I got my diagnosis and it was obvious I wasn't going to beat this thing, I knew what I wanted to do for you and your team. You guys didn't win a championship, but you were a huge reason why we won the championship a few years later. Without you and your team, we would never have won it. You committed and competed like champions, and you showed everyone what it would take to be a champion. You guys were part of every team I coached after you. You were committed like no other and I want to demonstrate one last commitment to you by

giving you this ring from our national champi-
onship. You are special, Tim, and so is your team.
You guys deserve it. You were the greatest team I
ever coached. Please receive it in memory of me
and be proud of the championship program we
built together. Remember, it's great to be here. I
love you forever!

Coach Richie

Tim opened up the small box and took the ring from the ring holder. He held up the ring and smiled. Even after he was gone, Coach Richie was still demonstrating his commitment to his team and creating a forever impact. It was as if he already knew the 7th Commitment. The ring didn't symbolize a championship for Tim. It symbolized how much Coach Richie valued and loved him and his teammates. Tim texted his teammates that he got a ring too and shared a picture of the card and the ring. It turned out that Coach Richie wrote each guy a handwritten note and engraved "Teammates Are Forever" inside each ring.

Later that evening, while looking once again at the handwritten card from Coach Richie, Tim remembered the time when he was a freshman and walked into Coach Richie's office and said, "I know I'm not playing well, Coach. I know I can play better. I'm going to play better. Just give me some time. I'll show you."

Coach Richie had told Tim to stop talking and politely walked him toward the door and said, "Kid, go to your dorm. Have a good night. We don't talk this game. We play it. Do it on the field." It was one of the greatest lessons Coach Richie ever taught him. The talkers talk and the doers do. Be a doer.

Tim made a commitment to himself and Coach Richie that he wasn't just going to talk about being a forever teammate and leader. He was committed to doing it and was going to do all he could to create a forever impact and help others do the same. He looked at the championship ring and had an idea. He wanted to create a reminder for his teammates and team members at work that symbolized the 7 Commitments.

After much thought and reflection, he had gold infinity pendants made, engraved with a small saying on the back: "It's great to be here." He sent them to his college teammates and gave one to all his employees, along with a card that listed the 7 Commitments.

The 7 Commitments of a Great Team

1. Commit to Valuing Each Other.

2. Commit to the Vision and Mission of the Team.

3. Commit to Staying Positive Together.

4. Commit to Giving Your Best.

5. Commit to Getting Better.

6. Commit to Connecting.

7. Commit to Each Other.

The End!

Book Resources

Get the 7 Commitments Action Plan

This downloadable plan is an accompaniment / implementation guide to help you take the principles from the book and turn them into action and results.

 www.7commitments.com

Access Tools / Exercises

Get access to tools and exercises shared in the book.

 www.7commitments.com/resources

Bring the 7 Commitments to Your Team and Others

» Workshops & Training – Our interactive programs will help your team embrace and apply the 7 Commitments for real, lasting impact.

» Keynotes & Leadership Events – Jon Gordon and our expert speakers bring the 7 Commitments to life with powerful insights and strategies.

Book a Workshop or Keynote →

🌐 jongordon.com/workshops

Get Certified & Lead the Change

Want to teach and facilitate the 7 Commitments training? Join the Jon Gordon Certified Trainer Program and get the tools, training, materials and support to share this message with others.

» Exclusive training & facilitation resources

» Official certification & branding

» Join a community of like-minded leaders

Become a Certified Trainer →

🌐 jongordoncertified.com

Reading this book is just the beginning. Let's make a greater impact, together.

STEP INTO POSITIVE LEADERSHIP-TAKE ACTION TODAY!

THE WORLD NEEDS MORE POSITIVE LEADERS. WILL YOU BE ONE OF THEM?

Negativity is everywhere. Leaders are burned out. Teams are struggling. The best organizations aren't waiting for change—they're creating it.

We're here to help you lead with vision, belief, and purpose so you can fuel your mindset, transform your leadership, and build a thriving team.

HOW YOU CAN GET STARTED TODAY

Start where you are—take the next step that's right for you.

1   GET FREE WEEKLY INSPIRATION

Start your journey with free, ongoing inspiration.

- **The Positive Tip Newsletter** – Weekly insights to fuel your mindset and leadership.

Subscribe Now →

🌐 www.jongordon.com/newsletter

- **The JonGordon Podcast** – Conversations with top leaders and thinkers.

Listen / Subscribe Now →

🌐 www.jongordonpodcast.com

2   EXPERIENCE OUR LIVE EVENTS

Join us for a wide range of exciting and exclusive events, both in-person and virtual.

» Interactive leadership experiences

» High-impact learning with Jon and top experts

» Networking with other high-performing leaders

Explore Events →

 www.jongordon.com/events

3   BRING JON GORDON'S TEAM TO YOUR ORGANIZATION

Want to train your team in the proven principles of positive leadership? Our expert facilitators will come to you—virtually or in person—to lead:

» The Power of Positive Leadership

» The Power of a Positive Team

» The Energy Bus Workshop

» Difficult Conversations Don't Have To Be Difficult

» The 7 Commitments of a Great Team

Book a Training →

 training@jongordon.com

4   BECOME A CERTIFIED TRAINER

Teach and facilitate Jon Gordon's leadership principles within your own organization or business.

» Certification to lead The Power of Positive Leadership, The Power of a Positive Team & The Energy Bus

» Exclusive facilitator resources, certification, and ongoing training

Become a Certified Trainer →

 www.jongordoncertified.com

5   JOIN JON GORDON'S CIRCLE (ELITE COMMUNITY)

The highest level of mentorship, coaching, and access to Jon Gordon and top leaders.

» Monthly live coaching calls with Jon

» VIP access to events & leadership resources

Apply for Jon Gordon's Circle →

 www.jongordoncircle.com

Take Action!

Whether you start small or go all in, taking action is what matters.

Your team needs leadership. Your organization needs positive change. We're here to help you grow.

☞ What will you do next?

Acknowledgments

I want to thank all the leaders, coaches, and teammates who made this book possible. You inspired, encouraged, and energized me. Without you this book wouldn't have been possible. I specifically want to thank Billy Donovan and Patric Young. Our conversations over the years were an instrumental part of this book and made it unique and meaningful. I want to thank all my college teammates, many whose names I used in the book for fun. I love that we are still friends after all these years. I want to thank Chad Busick for reading the book and sharing ideas that made the book even better. I want to thank the real-life coach Amy, Amy Kelly, my co-author of *Difficult Conversations Don't Have to be Difficult*. Our conversations about team building have sparked many ideas that have made our work more effective and impactful. I want to thank Damon West for the story about the best team-building strategy he had ever experienced. He told me that while I was taking a walk early in the writing process, and I immediately knew it would go toward the end of the book and lead to the 7th Commitment. I want to thank my home team, Kathryn, Jade, and Cole, for making me a better teammate. And I want to thank my team at John Wiley for helping me share this book with the world.

About the Author

JON GORDON is a 17-time bestselling author and thought leader, a top 3 leadership speaker, and a consultant who has worked with many of the top leaders and organizations on the planet. He is also a global influencer and inspirational teacher who impacts millions of people each year with his books, talks, podcasts, and messages.

Other Books by Jon Gordon

The Energy Bus

A man whose life and career are in shambles learns from a unique bus driver and set of passengers how to overcome adversity. Enjoy an enlightening ride of positive energy that is improving the way leaders lead, employees work, and teams function. **www.TheEnergyBus.com**

The Energy Bus Field Guide

Jon Gordon's international bestseller, *The Energy Bus,* has inspired thousands of businesses, organizations, sport teams, schools, and families alike, helping them cultivate positive energy, overcome adversity, and bring out the best in themselves and those around them. *The Energy Bus Field Guide* is a simple and powerful guide for putting *The Energy Bus* lessons to work. Using the 10 principles, you'll discover how to navigate the twists and turns that often sabotage individual and team success, and how to move in the right direction with vision, focus, purpose, and positive energy.

The Energy Bus for Schools

Based on *The Energy Bus,* the *Wall Street Journal* bestseller by lead author Jon Gordon, *The Energy Bus for Schools* teaches educators how to fuel their schools, themselves, and their students with positive energy. Research shows that culture and leadership greatly influence a school's learning environment and students' academic success. This book will help teachers work together to create a school culture where school leaders and students can grow into positive leaders, energizing their school culture as a united front.

The No Complaining Rule

Follow a vice president of human resources who must save herself and her company from ruin and discover proven principles and an actionable plan to win the battle against individual and organizational negativity.
www.NoComplainingRule.com

Training Camp

This inspirational story about a small guy with a big heart, and a special coach who guides him on a quest for excellence, reveals the 11 winning habits that separate the best individuals and teams from the rest.
www.TrainingCamp11.com

The Shark and the Goldfish

Delightfully illustrated, this quick read is packed with tips and strategies on how to respond to challenges beyond your control in order to thrive during waves of change.
www.SharkandGoldfish.com

Soup

The newly appointed CEO of a popular soup company is brought in to reinvigorate the brand and bring success back to a company that has fallen on hard times. Through her journey, discover the key ingredients to unite, engage, and inspire teams to create a culture of greatness.
www.Soup11.com

The Seed

Go on a quest for the meaning and passion behind work with Josh, an up-and-comer at his company who is disenchanted with his job. Through Josh's cross-country journey, you'll find surprising new sources of wisdom and inspiration in your own business and life.
www.Seed11.com

Other Books by Jon Gordon

One Word

One Word is a simple concept that delivers powerful life change! This quick read will inspire you to simplify your life and work by focusing on just one word for this year. *One Word* creates clarity, power, passion, and life-change. When you find your word, live it, and share it, your life will become more rewarding and exciting than ever.

www.getoneword.com

The Positive Dog

We all have two dogs inside of us. One dog is positive, happy, optimistic, and hopeful. The other dog is negative, mad, pessimistic, and fearful. These two dogs often fight inside us, but guess who wins? The one you feed the most. *The Positive Dog* is an inspiring story that not only reveals the strategies and benefits of being positive, but also an essential truth: being positive doesn't just make you better; it makes everyone around you better.

www.feedthepositivedog.com

The Carpenter

The Carpenter is Jon Gordon's most inspiring book yet—filled with powerful lessons and success strategies. Michael wakes up in the hospital with a bandage on his head and fear in his heart after collapsing during a morning jog. When Michael finds out the man who saved his life is a carpenter, he visits him and quickly learns that he is more than just a carpenter; he is also a builder of lives, careers, people, and teams. In this journey, you will learn timeless principles to help you stand out, excel, and make an impact on people and the world.

www.carpenter11.com

Other Books by Jon Gordon

The Hard Hat

A true story about Cornell lacrosse player George Boiardi, *The Hard Hat* is an unforgettable book about a selfless, loyal, joyful, hard-working, competitive, and compassionate leader and teammate, the impact he had on his team and program, and the lessons we can learn from him. This inspirational story will teach you how to build a great team and be the best teammate you can be.
www.hardhat21.com

You Win in the Locker Room First

Based on the extraordinary experiences of NFL Coach Mike Smith and leadership expert Jon Gordon, *You Win in the Locker Room First* offers a rare, behind-the-scenes look at one of the most pressure-packed leadership jobs on the planet, and what leaders can learn from these experiences in order to build their own winning teams.
www.wininthelockerroom.com

Life Word

Life Word reveals a simple, powerful tool to help you identify the word that will inspire you to live your best life while leaving your greatest legacy. In the process, you'll discover your *why*, which will help show you how to live with a renewed sense of power, purpose, and passion.
www.getoneword.com/lifeword

The Power of Positive Leadership

The Power of Positive Leadership is your personal coach for becoming the leader your people deserve. Jon Gordon gathers insights from his bestselling fables to bring you the definitive guide to positive leadership. Difficult times call for leaders who are up to the challenge. Results are the by-product of your culture, teamwork, vision, talent, innovation, execution, and commitment. This book shows you how to bring it all together to become a powerfully positive leader.
www.powerofpositiveleadership.com

Other Books by Jon Gordon

The Power of a Positive Team

In *The Power of a Positive Team*, Jon Gordon draws on his unique team-building experience, as well as conversations with some of the greatest teams in history, to provide an essential framework of proven practices to empower teams to work together more effectively and achieve superior results.
www.PowerOfAPositiveTeam.com

The Coffee Bean

From bestselling author Jon Gordon and rising star Damon West comes *The Coffee Bean*: an illustrated fable that teaches readers how to transform their environment, overcome challenges, and create positive change.
www.coffeebeanbook.com

Stay Positive

Fuel yourself and others with positive energy—inspirational quotes and encouraging messages to live by from bestselling author, Jon Gordon. Keep this little book by your side, read from it each day, and feed your mind, body, and soul with the power of positivity.
www.StayPositiveBook.com

The Garden

The Garden is an enlightening and encouraging fable that helps readers overcome the 5 D's (doubt, distortion, discouragement, distractions, and division) in order to find more peace, focus, connection, and happiness. Jon tells a story of teenage twins who, through the help of a neighbor and his special garden, find ancient wisdom, life-changing lessons, and practical strategies to overcome the fear, anxiety, and stress in their lives.
www.readthegarden.com

Other Books by Jon Gordon

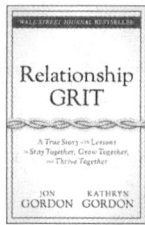

Relationship Grit

Bestselling author Jon Gordon is back with another life-affirming book. This time, he teams up with Kathryn Gordon, his wife of 23 years, for a look at what it takes to build strong relationships. In *Relationship Grit*, the Gordons reveal what brought them together, what kept them together through difficult times, and what continues to sustain their love and passion for one another to this day.
www.relationshipgritbook.com

Stick Together

From bestselling author Jon Gordon and coauthor Kate Leavell, *Stick Together* delivers a crucial message about the power of belief, ownership, connection, love, inclusion, consistency, and hope. The authors guide individuals and teams on an inspiring journey to show them how to persevere through challenges, overcome obstacles, and create success together.
www.sticktogetherbook.com

Row the Boat

In *Row the Boat*, Minnesota Golden Gophers Head Coach P.J. Fleck and bestselling author Jon Gordon deliver an inspiring message about what you can achieve when you approach life with a never-give-up philosophy. The book shows you how to choose enthusiasm and optimism as your guiding lights instead of being defined by circumstances and events outside of your control.
www.rowtheboatbook.com

The Sale

In *The Sale*, bestselling author Jon Gordon and rising star Alex Demczak deliver an invaluable lesson about what matters most in life and work and how to achieve it. The book teaches four lessons about integrity in order to create lasting success.
www.thesalebook.com

The One Word Journal

In *The One Word Journal*, bestselling authors Jon Gordon, Dan Britton, and Jimmy Page deliver a powerful new approach to simplifying and transforming your life and business. You'll learn how to access the core of your intention every week of the year as you explore 52 weekly lessons, principles, and wins that unleash the power of your One Word.

How to Be a Coffee Bean

In *How to Be a Coffee Bean*, bestselling coauthors of *The Coffee Bean*, Jon Gordon and Damon West, present 111 simple and effective strategies to help you lead a coffee bean lifestyle—one full of healthy habits, encouragement, and genuine happiness. From athletes to students and executives, countless individuals have been inspired by *The Coffee Bean* message. Now, *How to Be a Coffee Bean* teaches you how to put *The Coffee Bean* philosophy into action to help you create real and lasting change in your life.

The One Truth

In *The One Truth*, bestselling author and thought leader Jon Gordon guides you on a path to discover revolutionary insights, ancient truths, and practical strategies to elevate your mind, unlock your power, and live life to the fullest. Once you know the One Truth, you'll see how it impacts leadership, teamwork, mindset, performance, relationships, addictions, social media, anxiety, mental health, healing, and ultimately determines what you create and experience.

Success Journal

Success Journal: A Daily Practice for Positivity, Resilience, and Growth is a daily, lined journal where readers can write down their success of the day, shift their nighttime focus from negativity to positivity, and thereby create more success and opportunities in their lives. This resource is inspired by the legendary Bart Connor, who credited his overcoming a torn bicep muscle to win two gold medals at the 1984 Olympics to his parents asking him about his success of the day as a child.

Other Books by Jon Gordon

The Energy Bus for Kids

The illustrated children's adaptation of the bestselling book *The Energy Bus* tells the story of George, who, with the help of his school bus driver, Joy, learns that if he believes in himself, he'll find the strength to overcome any challenge. His journey teaches kids how to overcome negativity, bullies, and everyday challenges to be their best.
www.EnergyBusKids.com

Thank You and Good Night

Thank You and Good Night is a beautifully illustrated book that shares the heart of gratitude. Jon Gordon takes a little boy and girl on a fun-filled journey from one perfect moonlit night to the next. During their adventurous days and nights, the children explore the people, places, and things they are thankful for.

The Hard Hat for Kids

The Hard Hat for Kids is an illustrated guide to teamwork. Adapted from the bestseller *The Hard Hat*, this uplifting story presents practical insights and life-changing lessons that are immediately applicable to everyday situations, giving kids—and adults—a new outlook on cooperation, friendship, and the selfless nature of true teamwork.
www.HardHatforKids.com

One Word for Kids

If you could choose only one word to help you have your best year ever, what would it be? *Love? Fun? Believe? Brave?* It's probably different for each person. How you find your word is just as important as the word itself. And once you know your word, what do you do with it? In *One Word for Kids,* bestselling author Jon Gordon—along with coauthors Dan Britton and Jimmy Page—asks these questions to children and adults of all ages, teaching an important life lesson in the process.
www.getoneword.com/kids

Other Books by Jon Gordon

The Coffee Bean for Kids

The bestselling authors of *The Coffee Bean* inspire and encourage children with this transformative tale of personal strength. Perfect for parents, teachers, and children who wish to overcome negativity and challenging situations, *The Coffee Bean for Kids* teaches readers about the potential that each one of us has to lead, influence, and make a positive impact on others and the world.

www.coffeebeankidsbook.com